RIOJA

WINES OF THE
RIOJA

by **JAN READ** *with a foreword by Hugh Johnson*

Sotheby Publications

Frontispiece
The coopery at
Bodegas R. Lopez
de Heredia

In affection to
Antonio Larrea Redondo,
much loved and respected
in the Rioja,
and my first and
continuing mentor
in its wines.

© Jan Read 1984
First published 1984 for
Sotheby Publications by
Philip Wilson Publishers Ltd,
Russell Chambers, Covent Garden,
London WC2E 8AA

Available to the USA Book Trade from
Sotheby Publications
Harper & Row, Publishers, Inc.
10 East 53rd Street
New York, NY 10022, USA

Exclusive distribution to the Wine Trade
in the USA:

THE WINE APPRECIATION GUILD
155 Connecticut Street, San Francisco,
California 94107, USA
(415) 566-3532

ISBN 0 85667 186 X
Library of Congress Catalog Number 84-50546

Designed by Margaret Dodd of
Yellow Dog Graphic Works
Printed in Great Britain by Pitman Press, Bath

CONTENTS

*Old-fashioned
plough*

FOREWORD

Rioja has long been overdue for a worthy biography. Of all the regions that supply the world with truly distinctive wines up to the highest levels of quality it has had least ink lavished on it. Spaniards have been well aware of the province and its wines as their national Bordeaux and Burgundy for over a century. But to the wider world of wine-lovers Rioja really only made its debut in about 1970, and accurate detailed information about it is still scarce.

Happily the perfect biographer is at hand. There is no one who is even casually curious about Spanish wine who is not already in debt to Jan Read. In a series of books and articles over the last twenty years Jan has shared his ever-deeper knowledge of the whole of Iberia — not just its wines, but its history, its people, its monuments and cuisine — with a wide and respectful circle of readers. With his wife Maite, whose flair for tenacious investigation matches (sometimes even surpasses) his own, Jan has already become something of an institution: the first name you think of when a Spanish or Portuguese question needs answering.

To anyone who has had the pleasure of actually travelling with the Reads, as I have on two memorable journeys, the reasons are clear. Starting with a disciplined intellect (he is trained as a chemist), Jan made his living in the undisciplined, highly creative world of the movies. His film-scripts (of which *The Blue Lamp* is the most famous) are the work of a vivid imagination. So to Jan everything needs questioning, and every answer leads to new stories, new layers of information, new furniture for his formidably well-furnished mind.

This is the only way I can explain the sort of book this is. There have been monographs on wine regions, many on most regions, before. I don't think there has ever been one which has dissected its subject so neatly, analysed and described it so thoroughly or so precisely, put it together again so comprehensibly, and then breathed such life into the patient.

Hugh Johnson
January 1984

Traditional bodega with coat-of-arms over the door

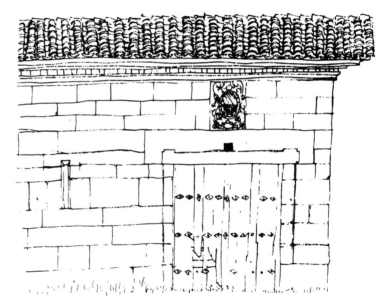

ACKNOWLEDGEMENTS

A host of wine-makers and wine merchants have helped in the preparation of this book; some I have thanked on previous occasions, but it would be churlish not to renew my thanks to some old friends and record the contribution of newer.

First are the official bodies in the Rioja: The Grupo de Exportadores de Vinos 'Rioja' and D. Carlos García-Ogara; the Estación de Viticultura y Enología in Haro and its Director, D. Manuel Ruiz Hernández, who has additionally allowed me to draw on his research papers; and the Casa del Vino in Laguardia and D. Fernando Martínez Bujanda. D. Antonio Larrea Redondo, former Director of the Estación de Viticultura has, as always, been a fund of information.

The *bodegueros* of almost all the concerns described in Chapter 6 have made me welcome in person. I should particularly like to thank D. Francisco Salamero Arrazubi of the Herederos del Marqués de Riscal and his sons, D. Fernando and D. Javier, who on several occasions invited my wife and myself to stay at their beautiful house and organized visits to other bodegas. D. Anastasio Gutierrez of R. López de Heredia, D. Isaac Muga of Muga, S.A., and D. Luis Vallejo and D. José Madrazo of C.V.N.E. are friends of such long standing that I should not *dare* to visit the Rioja without visiting them, picking their brains and tasting their wines.

New acquaintances who have been specially helpful are D. Javier Bilbao Iturbe of Bodegas Beronia, S.A., D. Luis Martínez Lacuesta Almarza of Martínez Lacuesta, S.A., and D. César Simon Echevarría, who has recently taken over at the Marqués de Murrieta from that doyen of Riojan oenologists,

D. Pedro-Jesús Marrodán Sainz. Apart from inviting me to visit his bodega, Sr del Milans de Bosch Solano of Bodegas S.M.S. showed me the old family house in Villabuena, as did the Condesa de Hernia her mediaeval castle, a gem of Riojan architecture, a photograph of which appears on p. 25.

Mr David Balls and Mr Jeremy Watson and their staff at Vinos de España in London have been of great assistance in arranging visits to the Rioja and in supplying statistical information. Mr John Hawes of Laymont & Shaw in Truro and Mr Barry Kettle of Arriba Kettle & Co. in Birmingham have been generous in supplying samples of the wines shipped by their companies; and without the sterling efforts of Mr Jeremy Bennet of London Wine Importers and Mrs Evelyn Ellis of Grants of St James's, and of Mr Graham Hines of Gonzalez Byass (U.K.) Ltd, the samples which we collected in the Rioja would never have been cleared by H.M. Customs & Excise.

I am indebted to *Decanter Magazine* and to its contributors, Mr Julian Brind M.W., Mr Clive Coates M.W., Mr Patrick Grubb M.W. and Mr David Scatchard for leave to reproduce the tasting notes on p. 119-21 and 135-7.

Except where otherwise indicated in the caption, the illustrations are reproduced from my own photographs. A number of photographs are reproduced by courtesy of Heraclio Fournier, S.A. D. Manuel Ruis Hernández and D. Luis Vicente Elias have kindly allowed me to reproduce various line drawings from their publications, and the sketch of Terete's restaurant in Haro is included by permission of Arriba Kettle & Co. of Birmingham.

Finally, I must thank most particularly Mr Hugh Johnson, a companion on various visits to the Rioja, both for supplying tasting notes and contributing the foreword to the book, and my wife, Maite Manjón, for her guidance on Spanish cooking and her support as an interpreter and taster.

INTRODUCTION

When I began writing a first book on Spanish wines in 1971 on the basis of a fair knowledge of what was available, an enthusiasm for things Spanish, a training as a research chemist — and the inestimable advantage of a Spanish wife who could talk to the *bodegueros*, few of whom spoke English, in their own language — my publishers came to the conclusion that the wines were so little known that I must also cover Portugal. It was only some ten years later that they judged the time ripe for a separate book on Spain; and now, in 1984, Messrs Sotheby's and Philip Wilson Publishers are adventurous enough to print a study of a single Spanish region!

A great deal, of course, has happened in the intervening period. There is general recognition abroad that Spain can provide something better than inexpensive 'plonk', though the occasional prejudiced and ill-informed columnist can still write that 'Spaniards obstinately continue with their barbaric methods to produce oceans of wine with unpronounceable names, from grapes which might pass muster as elderberries or brussels sprouts in any civilised country'. In actual fact, there have been striking advances in replanting with better grape varieties and the introducion of controlled fermentation and other modern methods of vinification.

Rioja is the best-known of Spanish table wines, and none has made more impact on foreign markets. Bare statistics tell a revealing story. In 1970, shipments of Rioja to the United Kingdom amounted to some 20,000 cases; by 1983, they had increased to around 350,000. Apart from energetic promotion by the former Rioja Wine Information Centre and its successor, Vinos de España, the main reason for this success is that, in the medium price range,

Riojas have provided an acceptable alternative to prohibitively expensive vintage wines from France. Over and above such good quality wine for regular drinking, connoisseurs have discovered that there are also old vintage Riojas which can hold their own with most.

The boom in exports of Rioja has posed its own problems to the producers. When I first wrote about the wines, most of them were made by medium-sized family firms and given long ageing in oak casks; this resulted in the 'vanilla' nose and flavour so attractive to their admirers, but criticized by others schooled in the classical French wines as masking the bouquet and flavour of fruit.

During the 1970s, a new generation of very large bodegas sprang up, equipped with the most modern plant and often owned by multi-nationals primarily interested in selling their wines abroad. An obvious step was to reduce the time in oak, so lessening the high costs of casks and of maturing the wines for excessive periods, and at the same time providing something of wider appeal abroad. In the case of the new-style white wines fermented at low temperature, ageing in oak has often been dispensed with altogether, both with the object of reducing costs and of making light, fresh, fruity wines of the type now generally popular.

The question is: has this process gone too far? For example, Mr David Wolfe echoes other professional tasters in saying at a recent *Decanter* tasting that: 'Too many makers are cutting down on the ageing period of their wines and only still manage to sell their wines because of the reputation Rioja enjoys. The types of Rioja we tasted today are merely hanging on the coat-tails of the better Riojas which have been aged for longer periods, for which the region was known in the past.'

He can be assured that the traditional bodegas, such as López de Heredia, Riscal, Murrieta, La Rioja Alta, C.V.N.E., Lacuesta and Muga, continue to make their wines as they always did; but the dilemma is a real one for the huge new industrial concerns, urged on the one hand to make less oaky wines, and on the other constrained to sell their wines at competitive prices in a cut-throat world market.

What has also led to some confusion are changes in the labelling of the wines. In the past there was an understanding that a *reserva* was a wine matured for not less than six years between cask and bottle, and a *gran reserva* a wine with not less than eight years' maturation. Under present regulations, a *reserva* need spend no more than one year in cask and two in bottle, and a *gran reserva*, two years in cask and three in bottle.

Adjustments to the production and labelling of the wines in conformity with the requirements of the E.E.C., which Spain in due course hopes to join, should not prove difficult; the wines exported to Common Market countries already conform to the Commission's regulations.

A more pressing problem is inflation, which has been increasing in Spain at no lesser a rate than in many of the countries with which she is competing, and recent reports indicate that the cost to the bodegas of co-operative-made wine of the 1983 vintage has in some cases increased by as much as 100 per cent. Foreign wine-drinkers will continue to buy Rioja as long as it represents good value, but may well revert to old favourites or turn to the wines from 'newer' producers such as California, Australia and Chile, if there is any steep rise in prices.

Given the dynamism of producers who are for the first time tapping world markets, confidence in what they are making, the quality of the grapes and the privileged geographical situation of the area, these are, I am sure, all problems which the Rioja will take in its stride.

ROUTES AND HOTELS

The quickest and easiest way to reach the Rioja is to fly to Bilbao and to hire a car from Avis, Hertz or one of the Spanish firms with desks at the airport. The drive by the A.68 *autopista* through beautiful, wooded mountains, takes about one-and-a-half hours to Haro or two hours to Logroño.

If you take your own car, there is an overnight ferry from Plymouth to Santander. It is then a question of driving the 109 km along a winding and much congested road, and joining the A.68 *autopista* outside Bilbao. Alternatively, of course, one may drive through France, crossing the border at Hendaye, proceeding via Irún, San Sebastián and Vitoria, and joining the A.68 *autopista* at Miranda del Ebro.

A car is more or less a necessity to explore the smaller places and outlying areas, such as the wooded heights and gorges of the Sierra de la Demanda, with the famous monasteries in its foothills. A good idea of the two western wine-growing areas, the Rioja Alta and Rioja Alavesa, may be obtained by taking the northern branch of the N.232 out of Logroño; following it through the wine townships of Laguardia, Abalos, San Vicente de la Sonsierra and Labastida in the Rioja Alavesa; crossing the River Ebro into Haro in the Rioja Alta, and following the southern branch of the road through Briones (leaving the main road to go up to the town for the magnificent view from its battlements) and the large wine-making centres of Cenicero and Fuenmayor back to Logroño. In all, this is a circuit of about 100 km.

Haro, a town with a population of some nine thousand, the wine capital of the Rioja Alta, is built on hilly ground overlooking the Ebro, and is the

*Cenicero from
Bodegas Riojanas*

home of some dozen of the best-known bodegas and also of the government wine laboratory (see p. 53). The centre, with its narrow streets, baronial houses and wide main square, preserves a lot of character. In the square, it is worth visiting the wine shop of Juan González Muga, which specializes in old and rare vintage wines from all over Spain and has 'special offers' of wines from the local bodegas. The 'wine museum' at Briñas on the way in from Labastida is an adjunct of a large bar-restaurant with a good distant view of the famous Conchas, and is of interest only because it exhibits bottles from almost all of the bodegas in the Rioja. Haro possesses two excellent restaurants described in Chapter 8.

A visit to the Rioja Baja from Logroño is most easily made by driving the 78 km in the opposite direction to Alfaro at its eastern extreme, branching off the A.68 *autopista* to look at vineyards and to see places such as Calahorra

The Conchas de Haro from Briñas

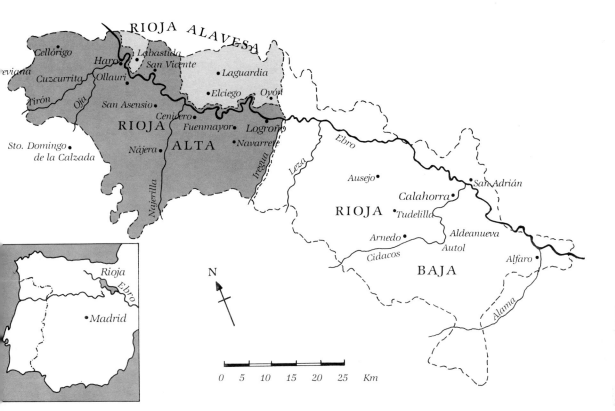

he Rioja

and the most picturesque town in the area, Arnedo, situated in the rocky
gorge of the River Cidacos. If approaching the Rioja from Barcelona by the
autopista via Zaragoza and Tudela, you will cover the same ground in a
westerly direction.

Even if you have a car, it is well worth taking the leisurely electric train
from Logroño to Haro. Unlike any of the roads, the line clings to the River
Ebro with superb views of the river, vineyards and hilltop towns; and the list
of stations — Fuenmayor, Cenicero, San Asensio, Briones and Haro — reads
like a wine merchant's catalogue. The journey takes about one hour, and the
train deposits you in the famous Barrio de la Estación in Haro, with bodegas
such as López de Heredia, La Rioja Alta, C.V.N.E. and Muga within a few
minutes walk. Should you wish to continue, another twenty minutes will
take you to Miranda del Ebro; and the train passes at water level through
the spectacular gorge of the Conchas de Haro. (The A.68 *autopista* follows
a much less scenic route some kilometres to the south.)

*The square
in Briones*

Visits may be paid to some of the larger bodegas, for example, A.G.E., Federico Paternina and Riojanas, without advance notice; but it is always better to telephone beforehand or to get the porter at the hotel to do this for you. In the case of smaller concerns, it is well to come armed with a letter from a shipper or wine merchant and to bear in mind that there may be nobody on the premises who speaks English.

For those who do not wish to make their own arrangements, or to drive, informative and enjoyable tours are available from time to time from specialist travel agents, notably Blackheath Travel, 13 Blackheath Village, London SE3 9LD.

The best centre for a visit, with numerous hotels and restaurants, is Logroño, roughly at the centre of the region. Haro possesses no good hotel, though romantics may like to stay in the atmospheric surroundings of the historic Parador in Santo Domingo de la Calzada, 15 km to its south. The charming Hostal de Samaniego in Laguardia, formerly installed in an old baronial mansion, no longer functions as a hotel, having been taken over as a wine institute. If you wish to make a stop-over in the Rioja Baja, there is the comfortable modern Parador of Marco Fabio Quintiliano in Calahorra, and hotels in Alfaro and Arnedo. Details follow; restaurants are listed in Chapter 8.

HOTELS

Logroño

**** *Carlton Rioja*, Gran Vía, 5; Tel. 24 21 00. Large and luxurious modern hotel, with *cafetería* but no restaurant.

*** *Murrieta*, Marqués de Murrieta, 1; Tel. 22 66 08. A favourite of the wine trade. Its large *cafetería* is a popular meeting place, and its restaurant, *El Figón*, is of good standard.

*** *Los Bracos*, Bretón de los Herreros, 29; Tel. 22 41 50. A modern hotel with *cafetería*, but no restaurant.

** *Gran Hotel*, General Vara de Rey, 5; Tel. 22 21 00. Old-fashioned and once the leading hotel in Logroño; without restaurant.

Santo Domingo de la Calzada (15 km south of Haro)

*** *Parador Nacional Santo Domingo de la Calzada*, Plaza del Santo, 3; Tel. 34 03 00. Installed in a mediaeval hospice for pilgrims, with magnificent arched hall and simple modern rooms. Regional dishes are available in the dining room.

Ezcaray (14 km south of Santo Domingo de la Calzada)

** *Cri-Crap*, Santo Domingo road; Tel. 35 40 00. On the mountainous southern fringe of the Rioja and off the beaten track, but close to the Monasteries of Suso and Yuso, this is a small and picturesquely-situated hotel with garden and restaurant.

Alfaro (78 km from Logroño in the Rioja Baja)

** *Palacios*, Zaragoza road, km 232; Tel. 18 01 00. Picturesquely situated, with a swimming-pool and a restaurant serving regional food.

Arnedo (49 km from Logroño in the Rioja Baja)

*** *Victoria*, General Franco, 113; Tel. 38 01 00. The best hotel in an attractive old town in the most scenic area of the Rioja Baja. With restaurant.

** *Virrey*, General Franco, 27; Tel. 38 01 50. With restaurant.

Calahorra (49 km from Logroño in the Rioja Baja)

*** *Parador Nacional Marco Fabio Quintiliano*, Era Alta; Tel. 13 05 38. Large and impressive modern Parador, with comfortable rooms and a restaurant serving regional food.

1 ORIGINS

The word 'Rioja' first appears in the Fuero de Miranda of 1092, one of the many local statutes to guarantee the rights of free men settling in territories recently recaptured from the Moors. It seems likely that, to begin with, the name applied only to the lands watered by the Rio Oja, a tributary of the River Ebro in the south-west of the present region; but before long it was being used for the whole rich agricultural basin of the Ebro from the rocky Conchas de Haro in the west to the flatter expanses of what is now known as the Rioja Baja, extending some 120 km to the east.

In his *Hand-Book for Spain*, the usually reliable Richard Ford wrote in 1845 that: 'this district, devoid of pleasure and interest, may fairly be blotted out of every traveller's map.' Perhaps he was influenced by the bad roads and uncomfortable diligences of the period, since it is a region of great natural beauty and historical interest. Bounded by the rugged Sierra Cantábrica to the north and the Sierra de la Demanda to the south, the valley is never more than 50 km wide, with the mountains, closer or more distant, forming a continuous backdrop to the patchwork of fields and vineyards. Through the centre, flows the Ebro, at times cutting its way between limestone cliffs and at others fringed by tall groves of Lombardy poplars; and always on the skyline is the profile of one of its hilltop towns — Briones, San Vicente de la Sonsierra, San Asensio, Laguardia and the others. Many of them were walled against the raiding Moors, and are dominated by an upstanding church, only too obviously a converted mosque.

The Rioja is a crossroads between the Basque country to the north and the mediaeval kingdoms of Castile to the south and west, and Navarra

*The River Ebro
near Briones,
with the Sierra
Cantábrica in
the background*

and Aragón to the east. It was a region much fought over in the past, and for much of the mediaeval period an integral part of Navarra; Nájera was, indeed, the second seat of the kings of Navarra, many of whom are buried in its monastery of Santa María la Real founded by García of Navarra in the eleventh century.

The first of the many waves of foreign invaders to penetrate the Rioja were the Phoenicians, whose traders pushed up the River Ebro in their shallow draught boats as far as Faro [modern Alfaro in the Rioja Baja], the site of the ancient lighthouse of Bilibio. During the early period, the most important town in the area was present-day Calahorra (the Calagurris of the Romans), whose blazon incorporates 'two naked arms fighting with swords, from which sparks issue', in reference to a vision said to have been beheld by Hannibal when he later captured the city. Of the accompanying motto, *'Prevaleci contra Cartago y Roma'*, Richard Ford comments that it is 'a modest untruth, seeing that the town was beaten both by Carthaginian and Roman'. After the eviction of the Carthaginians during the Second Punic War, the most stirring episode in Calahorra's history was its stubborn defence by the dissident Roman General Sertorius against the besieging army of Pompey the Great during his Spanish campaign of 76 to 71 B.C. Pompey was forced to retire after the loss of 3000 men, but four years later it was taken by Afranius after a siege in which, according to tradition, the defenders were reduced to such straits as for husbands to feed on their wives and for mothers to kill and salt their children, and to die rather than surrender.

Calahorra was the birthplace of Quintilian, critic, rhetorician and tutor of the Emperor Domitian's grand-nephews during the first century A.D. It was also the abode of Paulinus, a disciple of Ausonius, poet, wine-lover and Roman prefect of Gaul during the fourth century A.D. from whom the famous Château Ausone takes its name. Today, it is a placid, sunbaked place of mellow stone houses, the second city in the Rioja after Logroño, surmounted by a fine twelfth-century Romanesque cathedral.

Logroño, the capital of the Rioja and a city of some 85,000 inhabitants, was also well-established in Roman times, when it was known as Vera. Its

Fermentation chamber at the Roman winery near Funes

most distinctive feature is the wide, tree-lined Paseo del Espolón at the centre, where the festivities of the week-long fiesta of San Mateo, starting on September 21st to celebrate the beginning of the wine harvest, reach their climax. The home of several important bodegas, it is the headquarters of the Exporters' Association (the Grupo de Exportadores) and also the official controlling body, the Consejo Regulador de la Denominación 'Rioja'. Near the centre of the wine region, it is perhaps the best base for visiting the area.

During the pacification of Spain in the Augustine period, Roman troops were posted in strength around the area. Cenicero, now an important wine town, took its name from '*cenicero*' (meaning an 'ashtray') and is so called because the legionaries cremated and buried their dead on the site. Gimileo, near Ollauri, the birthplace of the famous firm of Paternina, is a corruption of 'Gemini', a name given to famous twin legions.

The Romans held sway in the Rioja, as in other parts of Spain, for some four centuries, until the first waves of 'barbarians' from the north entered Iberia via the Pyrenees during 407 to 409. Apart from the building of roads and bridges, administrative reorganization and the Christianization of the country, they revolutionized methods of agriculture and improved or planted vineyards wherever they settled. The remains of a large Roman bodega still survive at Funes, across the Ebro in Navarra, near San Adrián. It is difficult to find, as the site is unmarked but adjoins the C.115 just north of the bridge over the river. Effigies of the Emperors Domitian and Hadrian discovered on the site (and now in a museum in Bilbao) indicate that the winery was in operation during the latter part of the first century A.D. and the early years of the second. Four of the chambers were evidently used for crushing and pressing the grapes, and measurements of the fermentation troughs and storage vessels suggest that the capacity was of the order of a sizeable 75,000 litres.

It is difficult to say to what extent the production and consumption of wine was maintained during the three centuries of Visigothic rule that followed the crumbling of Roman Spain; but is seems likely that the Hispano-Roman nobility and the Romanized inhabitants of the cities lost none of their taste for it. It is certain that after the Moorish invasion of 711, viti-culture underwent a marked recession, though the more sophisticated of the invaders like al-Mu'tamid, the poet king of Sevilla, openly flouted the Koranic prohibition and even wrote verses in praise of wine. The following lesser-known poem by Samuel Ha-Nagid (903-1056), vizier of King Badis of Granada, is reproduced from David Goldstein's *The Jewish Poets of Spain* (Penguin Books, 1971):

*The Castle of
Torremontalbo
in the Rioja Alta*

Red in appearance, sweet to the taste,
Vintage of Spain, yet renowned in the East,
Feeble in the cup, but, once up in the brain,
It rules over heads that cannot rise again.
The bereaved, whose blood is mixed with his tears —
The blood of the grape demolishes his fears.
Friends, passing the cup from hand to hand,
Seem to be gambling for a precious diamond.

The period of Moorish domination and the early stages of Christian Reconquest were perhaps the most turbulent in the whole history of the Rioja. Pamplona fell to the Moors in 716 to 719, only a few years after their first landing in the Straits of Gibraltar, but Navarra and the Rioja in the north were distant from the centre of Moorish power in Córdoba. It was not long before the Beni Qasi family allied themselves with the local Basque potentates and set up as rulers in their own right and, as a consequence, the region was subjected to regular punitive raids or *sa'ifas* from the emirs and caliphs of al-Andalus.

In this lay the genesis of the mediaeval kingdom of Navarra which, as time went by, and the Christians of the north gained strength and confidence, joined forces with its neighbours in Aragón, León and Castile in the slow but relentless cause of Reconquest. It was at this period towards the end of the tenth century that the hilltop towns, such as Briones and San Vicente de la Sonsierra, were walled and fortified against perpetual Moorish incursions from the south. The most sizeable of these strongholds, the castle at Laguardia, a walled town of narrow alleys, old churches and underground wine-cellars crowning a hill some 20 km north-west of Logroño, was constructed for this purpose by King Sancho Abarca of Navarra (970-994), but was demolished in 1874.

An old vineyard near Cenicero in the Rioja Alta

However, to portray the fighting of the period as a war between Moors and Christians is greatly to oversimplify, since the Christian rulers of León, Castile, Navarra and Aragón were deeply divided and constantly at each others' throats. Sancho Garcés I (905-925) seized Nájera and the large part of the Rioja, and thereafter they remained part of the Kingdom of Navarra until occupied by Alfonso VI of Castile in 1076 and coming under the suzerainty of his favourite, García Ordóñez. Ordóñez was, however, the sworn enemy of another of Alfonso's erstwhile lieutenants, the famous El Cid, who descended on Logroño in 1092, razing the city to the ground.

Alfonso's annexation of Nájera opened up a new era in the relations of the Rioja, and indeed of Spain, with the outside world. The shrine of St James in Santiago de Compostela was becoming the object of a pilgrimage from all over Europe, and the route of the *Calzada*, or paved way, taken by the scallop-shelled pilgrims lay through Logroño, Nájera and Burgos. With King Alfonso's active support, a hermit, later to become San Domingo de la Calzada, bridged the rivers Najerilla and Oja, improved the old Roman road to Burgos and, in the town which now bears his name, built a hospice for pilgrims. Renovated as a Parador and close to Haro, it is now one of the most atmospheric of resting places when visiting the Rioja.

The original church used by St Dominic, raised to the rank of a cathedral in 1235, houses his tomb; and high on the opposite wall is a cage containing two live birds. These commemorate a strange legend. The hostess of a local inn was enamoured of a young pilgrim travelling to Santiago with his parents, and when he refused her advances hid some valuable goblets among his belongings. They were discovered, and the young man, less fortunate than Joseph, was hung from a gibbet. The bereaved parents, to whom he appeared in a vision, went to the *corregidor* and found him at dinner, only to be told that their son was as dead as the fowl on the table in front of him; at which point the birds sprang up and began singing. The young man was then discovered, still miraculously alive.

The wider importance of the pilgrimage and the *Calzada* was that it offered secure access to a country so long cut off from the rest of Europe; and some of the merchants and others who mingled with the pilgrims remained and settled in the towns along the route, forming small foreign colonies. In Logroño, some of the old houses of the *barrio de francos* (French Quarter) still survive.

It is perhaps not fanciful to suggest that these French immigrants helped to revive an interest in wine. Certainly the Benedictine monks from Cluny in Burgundy, who set up a network of churches, hospices and hospitals for the use of pilgrims, took a lively interest in viticulture if only to provide

wine for the sacraments; and the revival of wine-making in the Rioja is closely
associated with the three monasteries of San Millán de Suso, San Millán de
Yuso and Valvanera, lying within the triangle north of Nájera and Santo
Domingo de la Calzada. All are worth a visit.

The smallest and perhaps the most evocative of the three is San Millán
de Suso, perched high in the wooded mountains, with scenic views of the
great bulk of San Millán de Yuso in the valley directly below. Founded in
the tenth century on the spot where San Millán, to whose miraculous inter-
vention on the field of battle the Christians owed their legendary victory
over 'Abd al-Rahman III in 939', was born and died, it is Moorish in influence
with horseshoe arches and splendidly-carved Corinthian capitals. In one of
its small rocky recesses there is a reclining twelfth-century effigy of the saint.

San Millán de Yuso was founded in the eleventh century, but nothing
remains of the original building; and the crouching, rosy-coloured monastery
with its endless regularly-spaced windows resembles nothing so much as a
second Escorial, lying in a fold of the mountains, and dates from the seven-
teenth and eighteenth centuries. It contains wide courtyards, Gothic cloisters
and a sacristy which, with its guilded plasterwork vaulting, is one of the
most beautiful in Spain.

The Library is famous because it contains the first text to be written
in Castilian rather than Latin. In the early thirteenth century, it was a lay
brother of San Millán de Yuso who wrote one of the first poems in Castilian,
appropriately enough a eulogy of Rioja wine:

> . . . *En roman paladino*
> *en el cual suele el pueblo fablar a su vecino*
> *ca non soi tan letrado por fer otro latino*
> *bien valdra como creo un vaso de bon vino*

> . . . I'd like to write in the elegant prose
> Our forebears used, but heaven knows,
> I'm no scholar of Latin divine,
> So let's enjoy a glass of good wine.

The fifteenth-century Monastery of Valvanera, lying 1000 m up at the
top of the winding gorge of the River Najerilla in the Sierra de la Demanda,
was sacked and largely destroyed during the Peninsular War (1808-14). It is
only recently that it has been restored and reinhabited by the Benedictines.
Founded on the spot where a figure of the Virgin was miraculously discovered
in thick undergrowth, it once again houses the famous eleventh-century effigy
of the Queen and Patroness of the Rioja.

The seventeenth-century Monastery of San Millán de Yuso

It was in the shelter of these monasteries, high in the hills to the south of the Ebro, that the work of replanting the vines began. They were of the high-growing type, either staked or grown as they are to this day in Galicia and northern Portugal in pergolas. As conditions became more settled, vineyards were planted on the outskirts of the towns; and low-growing vines, often irrigated, made their appearance in the valleys of the Ebro and its tributaries. Unlike today, most of the wine made at this period was white; in a history of Haro, Domingo Hergueta notes that even in the sixteenth century 'La Ciudad de Jarreros' ('The City of the Jug-makers') made nothing else, and as late as 1609 Haro produced 32,266 *cántaras* (of about 32 pints) of white wine as against 6733 of red.

During the mediaeval period the main market for Rioja wines, outside the immediate area, was in the mountainous Basque country to the north. Their quality was indifferent: the wines are hardly mentioned by writers of the period and were rated much below those of Ribadavia in Galicia and of Toro, the prime favourites among the schoolmen of the University of Salamanca, but were much in demand in a region which produced nothing except for cider and the astringent chacolí, a young, *pétillant* wine containing only some 9 per cent of alcohol. Because of the prevalence of bandits on the steep and narrow roads to the north, the main staging-point was Vitoria to the west; and the wine was conveyed in mule-trains, together with other produce from the region such as wool, fruit and olive oil.

At the beginning of the sixteenth century, Bilbao became the main distribution centre, and its dealings in wine received a great fillip with the establishment, in the early eighteenth century, of the Compañía de Caracas, founded to trade Spanish wine for South American cocoa. With the setting up, later in the century, of the Compañía de Filipinas, prospects for the shipment of Rioja wines to foreign parts seemed bright, but proved short-lived — like the wines themselves; made by primitive traditional methods, they would not last for upwards of a year or a year-and-a-half and did not survive the long sea passage.

As early as the fourteenth centuries, it had been the practice to make a little 'clairet' ('claret'). So Henry Cock, a fourteenth-century English traveller, writes of La Estrella (a Hyeronimite monastery near San Asensio), that its 'wines, both the whites and clarets, are famous in the region, since they are not as thick and common as the others.' They were not, in fact, clarets in the modern sense, but '*blancos pardillos*', made by blending a little red wine with the white. The elaboration of light wines made by vinifying red and white grapes together was a later development and gathered impetus during the eighteenth century, both as a result of their popularization by the first of the Spanish Bourbons, Philip V, and a demand from Anglophile Bilbao for wines of the claret type, so favoured in England.

Meanwhile, a Royal Society of Harvesters of the Rioja had been formed by 1787 with the aims of expanding markets in the Basque country and improving the quality of the wines. A main objective was the improvement of communications with Bilbao and the north and the construction of a road westwards from Logroño to Haro. Works were interrupted by the outbreak of the Peninsular War; it was not completed until 1831, and good communications with Bilbao were not established until 1880 with the opening of the railway-line from Bilbao to Tudela by way of Haro, Logroño, and the wine townships of the Ebro valley.

The first significant step in improving the wines was taken in 1780 by Manuel Quintano, a native of Labastida in the Rioja Alavesa. Casks of oak, chestnut, eucalyptus and other woods had long been employed for the transport of wine, but not for making or elaborating it, and preservatives such as resins, brandy and isinglass were employed in attempts to prolong its life. Quintano was much impressed by reports of the new methods being employed by Châteaux such as Lafite, Haut-Brion and Margaux in Bordeaux, involving destalking of the grapes, vinification in wooden vats, removal of solid matter by racking and the maturation of the wine in oak casks disinfected by the burning of sulphur candles.

His brother, a Dean of Burgos Cathedral, suggested that he should visit Bordeaux in order to study the new methods on the spot; but Quintano, who served in the army, had been wounded in the leg during the siege of Gibraltar and was too lame to make the trip. He nevertheless encouraged a group of growers to experiment along French lines, and in 1795 the barque *La Natividad* sailed from Santander for the West Indies with a number of 960-litre barrels of the wine and 1500 bottles — the first consignment of its kind — all of which arrived in perfect condition.

Quintano's success nevertheless aroused the jealousy of other producers in the area, and the Mayor of Labastida refused to discriminate between the new-type wines and the ordinary growths of the district. Quintano protested that his wine, which he described as '*fino*' because it was fined with eggwhites, was of superior quality. The case was referred to the Consejo de Castilla, which in 1806 actually set the price of the '*fino*' below that of the traditional short-lived product. The outbreak of the Peninsular War put an end to his brave experiment, and further efforts to make improved wines by the new techniques were to remain in abeyance for another forty years.

2 PHYLLOXERA AND THE FRENCH

It is often said that French influence in the Rioja dates from the outbreak of the *phylloxera* epidemic in Bordeaux in 1867. This is an oversimplification. With the incidence in 1852 of that twin scourge, *oidium*, in the French vineyards, merchants from Bordeaux had already turned to the Rioja for wine; but even before this, enterprising growers in the region were looking to France for methods to improve their wines.

After Manuel Quintano's pioneering work came to an end with the onset of the Peninsular War, three decades were to go by, and it was as the indirect result of another war that experiments were resumed. Luciano de Murrieta fought on the side of the pretender to the Spanish throne, Don Carlos de Bourbon, and after the collapse of the first Carlist Rebellion, sought refuge in London between 1843 and 1848 with his compatriate the Duque de la Victoria. Impressed by the English taste for fine French wines, he decided to look into ways and means of improving viniculture in the Rioja, first going to Bordeaux to study up-to-date French procedures.

In 1850 he returned to Logroño, where it was then the custom to pour the wine through the streets in rivers to make space for the new vintage. Setting to work in the bodegas of the Duque de la Victoria, he ordered one hundred 72-litre casks from Bilbao and used them for a crucial experiment in shipping his carefully-made wine. Fifty of them, consigned to Veracruz in Mexico, were unfortunately lost in a shipwreck, but the other fifty arrived safely in Havana. The diplomatic presentation of one of the casks to the governor of the Island, Don José de la Concha, until then no lover of Rioja, set the seal of approval on the venture.

Later vintages won enormous acclaim at the 1857 Exhibition of Agriculture in Madrid; Don Luciano was created Marqués de Murrieta in recognition of his services and in 1872 acquired an estate at Ygay outside Logroño and began selling the wines, made in a newly-constructed bodega, under his own name.

Meanwhile, the onset of *oidium*, a cryptogrammic infection affecting the leaves of the vine, which oddly enough first broke out in a nursery in Margate and later crossed the Channel, had caused an influx of buyers from France in search of alternative supplies. From 1853 they descended on Haro in large numbers. They were interested not only in the alcoholic strength, but also in quality. It was no doubt this, together with Don Luciano's example, which in 1862 persuaded the Provincial Legislature of Alava to employ a *vigneron* from Bordeaux, Jean Pineau, to instruct the local growers in French techniques.

Establishing himself in Laguardia, Pineau doggedly trod the highways and byways of the Rioja Alavesa, seeking to interest and instruct the growers, but without success. The reasons for this lack of interest were probably

The original cellars of the Marqués de Murrieta in Ygay

because the existing wines found a ready market in the Basque country, and even more because the smallholders lacked the resources to invest in new equipment and to buy oak casks in large numbers. Pineau's contract was therefore terminated in 1868.

There were, however, more substantial and enlightened producers who had taken a lively interest in Pineau's teaching, among them the Marquesses of Berguenda, Terán and Riscal, and also Don Francisco de Paula, who obtained permission to bottle his wine in Vitoria, subsequently selling it at three times the normal price.

When Pineau was on the point of packing his bags for home, Don Camilo Hurtado de Amézaga, Marqués de Riscal, engaged him as administrator and set about the construction of a bodega planned along the lines of the most advanced in the Médoc.

Apart from the wines made by Don Luciano de Murrieta at the bodegas of the Duque de la Victoria from 1850 onwards, Riojas had traditionally been made by tipping the bunches of grapes, stalks and all, into a *lago*, a large cistern of stone or plaster-lined brickwork. They were lightly trodden by foot; tumultuous fermentation set in; and after about a week, the wine produced by this means, the so-called *vino de lágrima*, was run into a smaller cistern or *pila*. Eighty per cent of the grapes in the *lago* remained intact and were then thoroughly turned with a fork, when renewed fermentation began. The wine run off at this stage, the *vino de corazón* or *vino de repiso*, was considered to be the best — deeper in colour and stronger in alcohol than the *vino de lágrima* and at the same time with the freshness of a wine made from whole grapes. The process was (and still is, because it is still widely employed in small bodegas) a version of what is now known as *macération carbonique*. The final stage was to press the *marc* remaining in the *lago*. This was done several times, and the wine from the first pressing, rich in extract and tannin, was blended with the *vino de corazón*. The new wine was then run into *cuvas* (large oak barrels) to undergo slow secondary fermentation.

The methods used by the peasants for clarifying the wine were crude in the extreme, a favourite being to throw a skinned lamb or other beast into the vat (there are, of course, numerous stories of drunken soldiers falling into the vats during the Peninsular and other wars and improving the end-product!).

The traditional method (without such refinements!) is still employed in small bodegas and can produce attractive wines, though they suffer from low acidity and are short-lived. Attempts to prolong the life by the addition of pitch or resin have already been mentioned and date back to the Greeks and the Romans, but had obvious disadvantages in adulterating the taste. Bodegas Riojanas still make a proportion of its wines by the traditional method, but in this case longer life is achieved by blending it with wine made by the Bordeaux method, introduced to the Rioja by the Marqués de Murrieta and the Marqués de Riscal and now universally employed in the large bodegas. There has, however, very recently been renewed interest on the part of the large bodegas in 'new wine' made by the traditional bodegas; it is, in fact, distinctly reminiscent of Beaujolais Nouveau.

The lay-out of the new bodega, planned with advice from Pineau and constructed by the engineer Ricardo Bellasola after detailed investigation in Bordeaux, was closely modelled on the best French practice of the time and is shown opposite. All the vessels, including the fermentation vats, were made of oak. The grapes were first destalked and crushed, and the must, still containing most of the skins and pips, was pumped into the *cubas* or fermentation vats. After tumultuous fermentation had finished, the wine was run off the *marc*, which was then pressed, part of the dark press wine being blended with the rest, allowed to settle in capacious oak *tinas* and finally run into 225-litre oak *barricas* (also, because of their origin, known as *bordelesas*). The wine was clarified by repeated racking from the lees and transference to fresh casks, and lastly fined with beaten egg-whites.

Long after the Châteaux in Bordeaux had reduced the time of maturation in oak to some eighteen months, the bodegas in the Rioja continued to age their wines, both red and white, for long years in cask; and the oaky vanilla-like nose is still typical of the wines made by the more traditional bodegas today.

The best of the wines were bottled by hand at the bodega; and the original bottle-store at Riscal, protected by locked wrought-iron grills and containing examples of every vintage since 1860, still survives. However, it was not until later (see p. 39) that bottling at the bodega itself became general practice.

Although Luciano de Murrieta was the first to introduce these methods to the Rioja at the bodega of the Duque de la Victoria, the bodega of Riscal in Elciego constructed in 1868 was the first to be purpose-built along French lines, pre-dating the installations of Murrieta at Ygay by some four years.

Jean Pineau completed his work by planting Cabernet Sauvignon, Malbec and other French grapes in Elciego, but the yield was disappointing in comparison with that of the native Tempranillo, although Riscal has continued to grow Cabernet Sauvignon and to use a proportion of the must in its wines.

With the outbreak of *phylloxera* in France in 1863 and the subsequent destruction of 1,600,000 of the country's 2,500,000 hectares of vineyards,

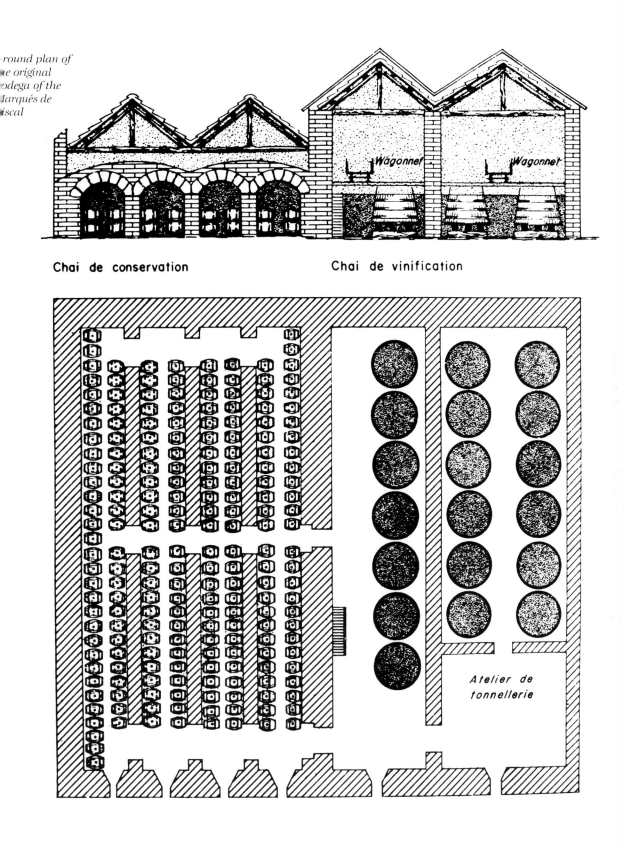

*round plan of
*e original
*odega of the
*arqués de
iscal

Chai de conservation   Chai de vinification

Atelier de tonnellerie

Contemporary engraving of the bodega of the Marqués de Riscal

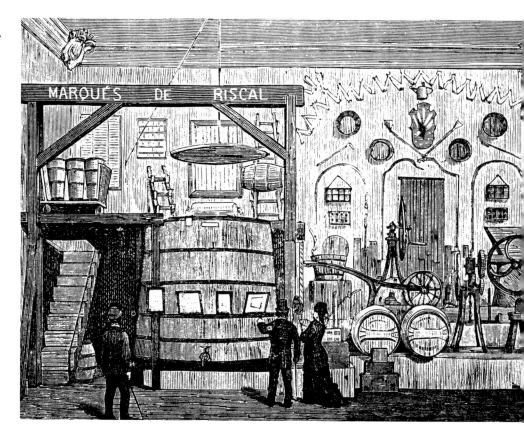

the French government drastically reduced duties on foreign wines, and by 1867, when the plague reached Bordeaux, the trickle of French *négociants* into the Rioja became a flood. To begin with, they limited themselves to buying and shipping wine, especially that from Elciego, Haro, San-Vicente de la Sonsierra, Briñas and Ollauri, establishing their depots around the station in Haro on the newly-opened railway from Bilbao to Logroño and Tudela. However, it was not long before they began constructing bodegas along Bordeaux lines to make the wine; and the Riojan wine-makers were to profit enormously from their example. Among the best-known were Alphonse Viguier, Philippe Savignon, François Blondeau, Charles Boisot, Eugène Krüger, Louis Parlier, Jules Leenhardt (the three last from Montpellier), and Armonde Heff (from Pau) — not to mention a glamorous widow, Catherine Joanne de Vandeben et Forseau who, however, soon sold her bodega and returned to her native Belgium.

A number of the most famous Rioja firms of today began operations in buildings taken over when their owners returned to France, or were founded by former employees of the French firms. Rafael López de Heredia bought the Haro warehouse of Armande Heff in 1881; Bodegas La Rioja Alta were founded by former Spanish associates of Alphonse Viguier; while Bodegas Franco Españolas were formed in 1901 by two well-known *vignerons* from Bordeaux, Federique Anglade and Alexandre Lepine, and Carlos Serres by another French merchant, Charles Serres. There were French technicians working at Bodegas Riojanas, constructed with advice from Bordeaux, until the outbreak of the 1939 War.

At the same time, some of the new bodegas set their sights higher than the production of table wines. Bodegas Bilbaínas, with headquarters in Bilbao, acquired a site near the railway station in Haro belonging to the French firm of H. Savignon et Cie and embarked on the production of sparkling wine by the Champagne process, and of brandy, both of which, together with table wines, it still makes today. Among the founders of the Compañía Vinícola del Norte de España (C.V.N.E.) in 1879 was a French *négociant*, Louis Perré, connected with Champagne establishments in Rheims and the cognac firm of Rémy Martin. It, too, established itself near the station in Haro and made *champaña* (as it might legitimately be called at the time) and also brandy, in a distillery at Alfaro in the Rioja Baja. So successful was its sparkling wine that a sister house was actually set up in Rheims. It survived for only three years, but C.V.N.E. long continued to supply the leading French Champagne-makers with Rioja wines at a period when they were experiencing difficulties with American grafts.

During the heady boom years of the late nineteenth century, when a monthly 500,000 hectolitres of wine were being shipped across the border, the Spanish government decided to annul the ban on imported cereals so as to encourage the plantation of vineyards. As a result, the cultivation of cereals was abandoned; olive-groves were cut down; and vines were planted even on the slopes of the Sierra Cantábrica.

In one respect the large new firms in Haro lagged behind the Châteaux in Bordeaux. It was their custom to bottle only small amounts of the best wines at the bodega—usually for very special clients, such as aristocrats and politicians—and the bottle were often enclosed in a fine wire mesh or *alambrado* to prevent fraudulent replacement of the contents. The practice survives, but more for decorative than practical purposes. The normal procedure was to ship the wine in cask by rail, and it was bottled in the cellars of the purchaser, a technician from the bodega accompanying each shipment with supplies of bottles, labels, corks and capsules. Many of the bodegas had private sidings and loading docks, but few now survive except for that at A.G.E. in Fuenmayor, where it is now used for the despatch of wine in bulk by railway-tanker.

There are examples of early bottled Riojas in the cellars of the Marqués de Riscal in Elciego and of Federico Paternina in Ollauri, many still in more than drinkable condition (see pp. 000 and 000). H. Warner Allen has written of one such wine in his *History of Wine*, (London, 1961) whilst describing the introduction of the bottle to Jerez:

> Elsewhere in Spain, as far as my knowledge goes, fine vintage wine is a rarity and I have only once experienced its possibility. That Prince of Hosts, Conde Antonio Osborne, at Puerto-Santa-Maria, the home of Fino Sherries, has inherited the literary tradition of Washington Irving, a Sherry lover, who dealt with the founder of his firm, and has opened for me the very last bottle of Rioja 1875 in his cellars. It has found a place among the memories which remain to me of very great wines, and I should like to think that such wines are still maturing in bottle, though here we shall never see them.

Later history has fortunately proved him wrong. I have myself drunk a magnificent 1920 Paternina, beautifully balanced, fruity and full of life, and 1917 and 1922 Riscals reminiscent of the best of St Émilions; and all vintage Riojas are now bottled in the bodegas.

The *phylloxera* epidemic broke out in the Rioja Alta in 1901-1902 and in the Rioja Baja in 1904-1905, with the severest damage in the Province of Logroño, where half the vineyards were wiped out. It had been preceded only a year or two before by the loss of the two last outposts of Empire, Cuba and the Philippines, two of the Rioja's most lucrative markets. By now, the new grafted vines in Bordeaux were in full production; the French government had doubled the duty on imported wine, and the abandonment of the Rioja by the French *négociants* and wine firms was complete. It was a dramatic progress from riches to rags.

Despite initial doubts as to the suitability of the most prevalent of the grapes, the Tempranillo, for grafting on to American stocks, the situation was restored, largely through the efforts of Francisco Pascual de Quinto, the agronomist appointed by the Provincial Legislature to supervise new plantations with American stocks.

Though a number of foreign administrators and oenologists remained with the large bodegas and the methods of making the wines were firmly rooted in experience gained from Bordeaux, French influence was henceforth to linger on only in the labelling of the wines with such fanciful names as 'Cepa Chablis' or 'Tipo Borgoña' and 'Tipo Burdeos' ('Burgundy-type' and 'Bordeaux-type') — the last two descriptions, in fact, referring to the body and depth of colour of the wines and being reinforced by their presentation in Burgundy bottles with sloping shoulders or the round-shouldered Bordeaux type.

The fortunes of Rioja and the French producers were to undergo another *volte face* with the outbreak of the 1914 War, when France was cut off from her foreign markets and the Riojans attempted to step in — with considerable success in America. However, the bodegas in Haro and elsewhere lacked the commercial expertise of the former generation of French *négociants* and further ran into difficulties over the supply of casks and bottles, and a more significant development was the setting up of offices in Madrid and Barcelona to meet the expanding domestic demand from restaurants and hotels.

The years between the two World Wars saw the establishment of further new bodegas, such as those of Berberana, Gurpegui and Enrique Bilbao, while others, like López de Heredia, C.V.N.E. and Paternina increased the scale of their operations, acquiring new vineyards and extending their bodegas. One of them, Bodegas Bilbaínas, established large cellars beneath the railway arches at Charing Cross Station to meet the growing demand for its wines in Britain.

Rioja was now becoming so well-known that it was found necessary to protect the name against fraudulent imitations, and a regulatory body, the Consejo Regulador, the first of its kind in Spain, was set up in 1926 (see also Chapter 3). Another development was the establishment of co-operative wineries, to which smallholders might bring their grapes to be vinified. Although they have not proliferated to the same extent as in some other parts of Spain, because of the existence of so many large commercial bodegas buying fruit directly from independent farmers, thirty survive and flourish. Among the best are the Co-operative of Labastida in the Rioja Alavesa, which both matures its wines in cask and bottles them, and Santa Daría in Cenicero, the main supplier of red wine for the excellent Marqués de Cáceres.

The Spanish Civil War of 1936-1939 caused widespread disruption in the bodegas, some of them virtually suspending operations; and in its wake, a general food shortage led to the uprooting of vineyards and the planting of wheat. Bread was a necessity, and wine a luxury. However, conditions were gradually restored, and the bumper vintage of 1970, rising living standards and increased demand for the wines from abroad, resulted in a flurry of activity reminiscent of the boom years of the late nineteenth century. Large new vineyards, such as those of Pedro Domecq in the Rioja Alavesa and Berberana in the Rioja Baja, were planted; old firms, such as Azpilicueta,

Finca *in the vineyards of Bodegas Alavesas in the Rioja Alavesa*

Montecillo and Santiago, were taken over by the Spanish banks, sherry firms and international wine and spirit combines; and a new generation of huge modern bodegas sprang up, some of them, like Lan and Olarra, financed by Spanish industrialists from other spheres.

The most ambitious of the new organizations moving into the area was the great R.U.M.A.S.A. conglomerate, embracing banks, hotels and heavy industry, in addition to interests in wine covering the whole country. Before its collapse and expropriation by the government in 1983, it had acquired the major concerns of Federico Paternina (of which control had long since passed from the Paternina family to a financial consortium in Bilbao), Bodegas Franco Españolas, Lan and Berberana; and there were fears among the more traditional *bodegueros* that it might soon engulf half of the Rioja, repeating its history in Jerez.

Another recent trend has been the construction of new medium-sized bodegas, making wine by strictly traditional methods, but at the same time taking advantage of modern techniques, of which happy examples are Bodegas Muga in Haro and Bodegas Beronia in Ollauri.

Although many connoisseurs of Rioja consider that the best wines are still those of the traditional bodegas, like Riscal and Murrieta and the small group founded in the Barrio de la Estación in Haro in the late nineteenth century, the new bodegas, with their stainless-steel fermentation tanks and provision for the 'cold fermentation' of white wines, have undoubtedly provided a stimulus to producers in the region as a whole. The old-established Estación de Viticultura y Enología in Haro and the elaborately-equipped Casa del Vino, recently set up in Laguardia to advise and assist smaller producers in the Rioja Alavesa, have provided valuable technical back-up; and now that the wines are being matured for a rather shorter period in oak and sold with adequate bottle age, the image of the Rioja as an old-fashioned and excessively oaky wine is changing and it is well able to compete with the best from other countries.

3 LEGISLATION AND LABELLING

Regulation of the trade and quality of wines in the Rioja area has existed since early mediaeval times. For example, a Royal Decree of 1255 laid down that:

> It is forbidden to sell a wine made by blending two different wines; nor may chalk, salt or any ingredient injurious to human consumption be added on pain of paying a fine of 60 *sueldos* or confiscation of the wine, half going to the King and the rest to the faithful.

However, the main bone of contention was the sale of wine from Navarra to the neighbouring areas of Castile, and the tenour of repeated *cédulas* (or Royal Decrees) from the period of Alfonso XI (1312-1350) onwards was protectionist. So, Alfonso decreed that:

> In the public interest we order that now and in the future the inhabitants of Vitoria and all other regions in our Realm be forbidden to bring wine from Navarra or any other place outside our Realm, nor may they go to fetch it or receive it.

The people of Vitoria were, in fact, no friends of the Riojans or their wines and openly flouted the regulations, setting on the muleteers from Logroño and slashing their wine-skins in the manner of Don Quixote. It was not until the advent of the Catholic Monarchs, who proved staunch supporters of the Riojans, that the laws were more rigorously enforced. They began by clearing the highways of bandits and, in response to pleas from Logroño, promulgated a Royal Decree in 1490 providing for the *Corregidor* of Logroño to inform the Council of State of shipments of wine from Navarra, so that effective action might be taken to defend the interests of the towns of Santo Domingo de la Calzada, Nájera, Haro and Navarrete, in common with others in the region.

With the help of measures such as these, the wine industry grew and flourished. A major preoccupation of the civic authorities in Logroño was the disturbance of the bodegas and their precious contents by traffic through its narrow streets. So, in 1596, the City Council decreed that: 'Because of the great damage done by carts with iron-shod wheels both to the streets and bodegas, resulting in costly damage and expense both in the streets and bodegas, we have agreed and decree that no vehicles with iron-shod wheels may proceed through the streets of the city under penalty of a fine of two thousand maravedís.'

In 1635, the *Alcalde* (Mayor) went even further, totally banning the passage of horse- and mule-drawn vehicles through the streets adjacent to the bodegas 'for fear that the vibration of these vehicles in the streets might affect the musts and thus influence the maturing of our precious wines.'

During the late nineteenth century, when wine could so easily be sold in France, the producers felt little need for protection; but, as the *phylloxera* epidemic receded and the French reinstituted tariff barriers, the problem re-emerged. The first step towards systematic legislation patterned on the French model was a Royal Decree of May 16th, 1920, defining 'origin' as applied to Rioja wines. In 1925, Primo de Rivera authorized the marking of Rioja wines with the modern seal; and a Consejo Regulador was established in 1926 with the objects of defining the boundaries of the region, controlling the issue of seals to the producers and taking legal action against fraudulent use of the name 'Rioja'.

At this point the historic feud between the Rioja and neighbouring Navarra resurfaced. Since the wines from both areas were broadly similar in character and the larger firms in Haro, Logroño and Elciego had for long been buying wine for blending from as far afield as Olite and Tudela, it would have been logical to incorporate much larger areas of Navarra than the narrow strip north of the Ebro now included in the demarcated area.

Further than this, the sub-regions in the present demarcated zone by no means correspond to well-defined organoleptic differences in their wines. To achieve good balance, the Graciano and Mazuelo from the Rioja Alta call for admixture with the fruity Tempranillo from the Rioja Alavesa, and, especially in poor years, for the body and alcoholic degree of the Garnacho from the Rioja Baja. The sub-regions are therefore interdependent; and there was no good reason for excluding further areas of Navarra — except that the bulk of municipalities in Navarra feared the loss of traditional and statu-tary rights by joining in the larger entity.

In the event, the first Consejo Regulador of 1926 proved singularly ineffective and gave way to a second in 1944; but it was not until 1953 that yet a third remodelled Consejo, armed with adequate legal powers, was to exercise effective control. Since 1972, it, like the Consejos Reguladores later formed in other regions, has operated under the overall control of the Instituto Nacional de Denominaciones de Origen (I.N.D.O.), set up by the Spanish Ministry of Agriculture.

The Consejo Regulador de la Denominación de Origen 'Rioja', to give it its full name, operates from Logroño and is headed by a President nomi-nated by the Ministry of Agriculture and a Vice-President named by the Ministry of Commerce. It further numbers five members representing the growers, one each from the three sub-regions and two from the co-operatives, and five representing the bodegas and shippers. Two further members, one of them usually the Director of the Estación de Viticultura y Enología (the Government Wine Laboratory), are appointed by the Ministry of Agriculture because of special knowledge of viticulture and oenology. An inspectorate attached to the administrative staff of the Consejo carries out regular checks in the vineyards and at the bodegas, working in col-laboration with the Estación de Viticultura y Enología (see p. 53).

The members of the Consejo do not always see eye to eye, since the farmers are concerned with fixing the best possible price for their grapes, whereas the bodegas and shippers are concerned with making and marketing wine that they can sell in highly competitive markets at home and abroad. Nevertheless, the basic object of the Consejo is to ensure that the wine pro-duced in the area is well-made and to provide a guarantee of quality to the consumer.

Apart from keeping detailed records of the production and elaboration of wines of different category and issuing back labels and seals to cover the amounts, the work of the Consejo centres on the implementation of regulations with which a wine must conform to obtain *Denominación de Origen* (D.O.), corresponding to the French *Appellation d'Origine Contrôlée* (A.O.C.) or Italian *Denominazione di Origine Controllata* (D.O.C.) and formu-lated in accordance with the rules of the Office International du Vin (O.I.V.).

The regulations fall under two heads, those of the *Estatuto de la Viña. del Vino y de los Alcoholes*, a government decree promulgated in 1970 and applying to Spain as a whole, and the more detailed provisions of the *Reglamento de la Denominación 'Rioja' y de su Consejo Regulador*, framed within the context of the *Estatuto*, but applying only to the Rioja regions.

The *Estatuto*, a lengthy document running to 134 *artículos* and some 20,000 words, embodies definitions of the different types of wines and alcoholic beverages, and detailed rules for acceptable and unacceptable methods of viticulture, vinification and chemical composition, together with regulations covering records of production and the transport, distribution, sale and export of wines. It draws a distinction between the grafting of shoots of the native varieties of *Vitis vinifera* on to American stocks — now generally employed — and the hybridization of American and native vines by cross-pollination, which is forbidden. There is a ban on the irrigation of vineyards, once traditional in parts of the Rioja — an embargo patterned on French practice and questioned by growers who point to its benefits in comparable areas such as California and Australia.

The provisions of the *Reglamento*, specific to the area, amount ultimately to restrictive measures designed to prevent the production of inferior wines and are more rigorous in the Rioja with its traditionally high standards than in many of the other demarcated regions. Again, the *Reglamento* of 1976 is a voluminous document, running to some 12,000 words, 52 *artículos* and hundreds of sub-sections, so that only some of the more important sections can be outlined.

In the first place, it defines the three sub-regions of the Rioja Alta, Rioja Alavesa and Rioja Baja and lists the municipalities of the *zona de produccion* as follows:

Rioja Alta

Abalos, Alesanco, Alesón, Anguciana, Arenzana de Abajo, Arenzana de Arriba, Azofra, Badarán, Bañares, Baños de Río Tobía, Baños de Rioja, Berceo, Bezares, Bobadilla, Briñas, Briones, Camprovín, Canillas, Cañas, Cardenas, Casa Arreina, Castañares de Rioja, Cellórigo, Cenicero, Cidamón, Cihuri, Cirueña, Cordovín, Cuzcurrita de Río Tirón, Daroca de Rioja, Entrena, Estollo, Foncea, Fonzaleche, Fuenmayor, Galbarruli, Gimileo, Haro, Hervias, Herramélluri, Hormilla, Hormilleja, Hornos de Moncalvillo, Huercanos, Lardero, Leiva, Logroño, Manjarrés, Matute, Medrano, Nájera, Ochánuri, Ollauri, Rodezno, Sajazarra, Sotés, Tirgo, Tormantos, Torremontalvo, Treviana, Tricio, Uruñuela, Ventosa, Villalba de Rioja, Villar de Torre, Villarejo, Zarratón and 'El Ternero'.

Rioja Alavesa

Baños de Ebro, Barriobusto, Cripán, Elciego, Elvillar de Alava, Labastida, Labraza, Laguardia, Lapuebla de Labarca, Lanciego, Leza, Moreda de Alava, Navaridas, Oyón, Salinillas de Buradón, Samaniego, Villabuena de Alava and Yécora.

An old street in Haro

Bridge over the River Ebro at San Vicente de la Sonsierra, with the Rioja Alta in background

Vineyards near Logroño

Rioja Baja

Agoncillo, Albeida, Alberite, Alcanadre, Aldeanueva de Ebro, Alfaro, Andosilla, Arnedo, Arrúbal, Ausejo, Autol, Azagra, Bergasa, Bergasilla, Calahorra, Clavijo, Corera, El Redal, El Vilar de Arnedo, Galilea, Grávalos, Lagunilla de Jubera, Mendavia, Molinos de Ocón, Murillo de Río Leza, Nalda, Ocón (La Villa), Pradejón, Quel, Ribafrecha, Rincón de Soto, San Adrián, Santa Engracia de Jubera (zona Norte), Sartaguda, Tudelilla, Viana and Villamediana de Iregua.

Separate zones are laid down for the maturation of the wines. These are:

Rioja Alta

Abalos, Briones, Cenicero, Cuzcurrita de Ŕio Tiron, Fuenmayor, Gimileo, Haro, Logroño, Navarrete, Ollauri, San Asensio and San Vicente de la Sonsierra.

Rioja Alavesa

Baños de Ebro, Elciego, Labastida, Laguardia, Lanciego, Lapuebla de Labaraca, Oyón, Samaniego and Villabuena.

Rioja Baja

Alcanadre, Aldeanueva de Ebro, Alfaro, Andosilla, Arnedo, Ausejo, Autol, Calahorra, El Villar de Arnedo, Murillo de Río, Leza, Quel, San Adrián and Tudelilla.

The seven permitted varieties of grape are described on pp. 66-70. For the red wines they are the Tempranillo, Garnacho, Mazuelo and Graciano; and for the whites, Viura, Malvasía and Garnacho blanco. Of these, the preferred varieties are the red Tempranillo and white Viura.

The density of plantation must lie between 3000 and 3600 plants per hectare, and the maximum permitted yields are 60 and 90 *quintales métricos* (1 *quintal métrico* = 100 kg) per hectare for black and white grapes respectively. Pruning must be by the traditional method of *poda en vaso* (see p. 75), but it is within the discretion of the Consejo to authorize new viticultural techniques, such as the staking and wiring of vines in Bordeaux fashion, when it considers that these will not prejudice the quality of the wines (it also countenances the use of Cabernet Sauvignon grapes, for long grown in the area in small amounts).

Turning to vinification and elaboration, the yield must not be more than 70 litres of must from 100 kg of grapes, and the name of the sub-region may not appear on the label unless all the grapes proceed from the sub-region and the wine has been vinified, matured and bottled there.

Unacceptable defects and adulterants, as also the permissable content of sulphur dioxide, are detailed in the *Estatuto;* as regards alcohol content, the Reglamento establishes the following limits:

	Minimum alcoholic degree (% by volume)
Rioja Alta	
Red, rosé and white	10°
Rioja Alavesa	
Red	11.5°
Rosé and white	11°
Rioja Baja	
Red	12.5°
Rosé and white	12°

Volatile acidity (expressed as acetic acid) may not exceed 0.2 g/litre for wines below 11°, 0.7 g/litre for wines between 11° and 13°, 0.8 g/litre for those above 13° and 1.2 g/litre for *crianza* wines (see p. 51).

The Consejo Regulador maintains registers of:

1 Vineyards, with details of their location, extent and characteristics.
2 *Bodegas de Elaboración* (wine-making establishments).
3 *Bodegas de Almacenamiento* (establishments for the storage and blending of wine with *Denominación de Origen*).
4 *Bodegas de Crianza* (establishments for maturing D.O. wines).
5 Exporters.

In the interests of maintaining quality and so as to ensure that the finer wines are made in establishments with sufficient resources to mature them in oak for the required period, only bodegas with 2250 hl or more wine in the process of ageing, at least half of it in a minimum of five hundred of the standard 225-litre oak casks, qualify for registration as *Bodegas de Crianza.* Similarly, concerns authorized to export their wines under the name 'Rioja' must possess a minimum storage capacity of 7500 hl. In contrast to a region like Bordeaux, with its hundreds of small and individual Châteaux, the effect of this legislation has been to limit the number of exporters to some fifty large or medium-sized firms. Some, like Campo Viejo (see p. 116) or Paternina (see p. 117), have a storage capacity of more than 50,000 hl.

As regards the different categories of wine, the traditional method of indicating age, still widespread in Spain itself, was to label it with a description such as '4° año', meaning that the wine had been bottled during the fourth calendar year after the harvest (a 2° año wine, harvested and vinified in October, is not, therefore, two years old, as is commonly thought, but nearer *one* year in age). The disadvantage of this method is that it gives no clue as to the actual year of vintage or as to how long the wine has spent in bottle. It reflects the stress laid on age in cask in a region where vintages tend to be fairly consistent. In the past it was left largely to the customer to age the wine in bottle, and it is only comparatively recently that the benefits of bottle age have been fully appreciated.

The Consejo Regulador first modified this system by stipulating that small back labels be attached to bottles, indicating whether the wine was '*sin crianza*' (without ageing) or '*con crianza*' (with ageing). Both types qualify for *Denominación de Origen* and carry the Rioja seal on the bottle, but the *Reglamento* requires that *crianza* wines, both red and white, 'must be aged for not less than two calendar years, of which one at least must be in oak casks of 225 litres'.

The *Reglamento* contains no definition of the terms '*reserva*' and '*gran reserva*', but in the past there was a gentleman's agreement with the *bodegueros* in the Rioja that *reservas* should be not less than six years old, and *gran reservas* eight years old. However, in August 1979 a separate *Reglamento de las indicaciones relativas a la calidad, edad y crianza de los vinos* was promulgated, applying to Spain as a whole.

This defines a *reserva* as wine of good quality, aged, in the case of the *tinto* (red) and *clarete* (light red), for at least three years between oak cask and bottle, with a minimum of one year in cask. White and rosé *reservas*

The modern Rioja seal

must be aged for at least two years between oak cask and bottle, with a minimum of six months in oak. *Gran reservas* are defined as wines of good quality, aged, in the case of *tinto* and *clarete*, for at least two years in oak cask, followed by a minimum of three in bottle. White and rosé *gran reservas* must be aged for a minimum period of four years, with at least six months in oak.

For an interim period these regulations were varied in the Rioja, where long ageing in oak has been the rule of the day and is indeed the very hallmark of traditional red Riojas; and the ruling of the Consejo Regulador was that red *reservas* must spend at least two years in 225-litre oak *barricas* and one in bottle, and the *gran reservas* at least three years in *barrica* and two years in bottle, with a minimum period of seven years in the bodega before release. However, the Rioja has very recently fallen into line with the rest of Spain.

At this point, the Consejo Regulador introduced two new back labels — for *reservas* and *gran reservas* as newly-defined (though it should be noted that some of the older *reservas* still carry back labels reading '*vino de crianza*'). These *reserva* wines are not as mature as those formerly so-labelled, corresponding to what was formerly thought of as a wine of intermediate age and labelled '4° or 5° año', and have given rise to complaints that they lack the characteristic oaky flavour of the past.

Again, in practice, the description '*vino de crianza*' is now largely confined to young 3° año wines, and not applied to 4° año and 5° año wines, which may now be called *reservas*. It should, however, be noted that the old-established firms continue to mature their *reservas* and *gran reservas* in cask for much longer than the minimum periods required by the Consejo Regulador.

All wines sent for export must now be labelled with the year of vintage. Certain of the well-known bodegas have always labelled their fine wines in this way, but the printing of a vintage year often implied (and the Rioja has not been alone in this) that the wine contained a preponderance of that of the stated year since, from the days of the French *négociants*, it has been the practice to blend wines from poor and scant years with those from better and more prolific so as to maintain consistent style and quality. It is, for example, difficult to believe that some of the seas of wine labelled as '1970' contain more than a modicum of that now near-legendary vintage. It is now mandatory for the bottle to contain 85 per cent of the vintage stated on the label, the only wine that may be blended with it being that of a younger vintage. This is no window-dressing formula, since the inspectors from the Consejo keep a strict record, bodega by bodega, of the wine produced in a particular year and are prompt to jump on offenders attempting to sell more wine of the vintage than they are on the books as having made or bought.

The practice of *coupage* or blending had died hard, and during the 1960s, when there was a shortfall of white grapes in the Rioja, the Consejo Regulador actually countenanced the import of white wine from other regions (mainly La Mancha), a '*canon*' or tax being levied on them and applied to the plantation of white grapes in the Rioja. It is now illegal to make wine with anything except grapes grown in the demarcated area, and the penalties for doing so are stiff, ranging from heavy fines to suspension.

Another practice outlawed by the Consejo is, of course, the use of oak chips or essences to confer flavour on the wines as a short cut to ageing them in oak. This was an issue which achieved considerable notoriety some years ago, with rumours of the surreptitious delivery of oak essence from Barcelona to wayside stations, but without any hard evidence being produced. It is something which it is impossible to detect by laboratory techniques such as gas chromatography, since the curves resulting from the use of oak essence and from ageing the wine in new oak casks are to all intents and purposes identical. Indeed, it is difficult to believe that it occurs at all in view of the rigorous inspection and recording of stocks of maturing wine by the Consejo; it also makes nonsense of the huge purchases of oak *barricas* by the new bodegas. Questioned about it, Don Manuel Ruiz Hernández, Director of the Estación de Viticultura, was of opinion that the *canard* had arisen simply because of the pungent oaky flavour conferred on the wines by the new casks of some of the newly operational bodegas.

Sparkling wines, made in small amount in the Rioja, do not come within the purview of the Consejo Regulador for the Rioja, but are made in accordance with a separate *Reglamento* first promulgated in 1972 and applying to Spain as a whole.

ESTACION DE VITICULTURA Y ENOLOGIA

Over the years the government wine laboratory in Haro has played a central part in the enforcement of the *Reglamento* by the Consejo Regulador and, perhaps as or more important, in helping the growers and *bodegueros* over their day-to-day problems and in disseminating up-to-date information about the techniques of wine-making. In this latter role, it has recently been joined by Casa del Vino in Laguardia, an agency of the Provincial Legislature of Alava, especially formed to assist the small producers in the Rioja Alavesa and to make available to them the most modern investigational and analytical techniques. Looking at its brand new equipment, one might easily imagine oneself to be at Davis University in California!

The first step towards the creation of an Estación Enologica in Haro, as it was first called, was a Royal Decree issued by Queen María Cristina in 1888, calling for the establishment of oenological stations in Alicante, Ciudad Real, Logroño and Zamora, with a central station in Madrid. It was a much-needed move, since at the time there was widespread ignorance about wine-making procedures, and much Spanish wine was badly-made and verging on the undrinkable. However, the decree provoked energetic protest from Haro, which regarded itself as the wine-making centre of the Rioja, and was replaced by a further decree on 1892 couched in more politic terms:

> *Article 1*   A central oenological station is to be created in the Alfonso XII Agricultural Institute [in Madrid], and others in the wine regions which the Government considers to be of most importance.

The *jarreros* ('jug-makers') of Haro had meanwhile been threatening to petition for secession from the Province of Logroño and incorporation in Burgos if the station did not come their way; and in March 1892 it duly opened its doors in a house in the Calle del Portero. It now operates from more spacious premises with well-equipped laboratories and cellars in a quiet *cul-de-sac* near the bullring.

Most illustrious of its early Directors was Don Victor Cruz Manso de Zúñiga, who held sway from 1893 to 1921. It was he who sounded the alarm in 1899 when *phylloxera* first appeared in the Rioja in the vineyards of Sajazarra and stemmed the invasion by the introduction of grafting on to American stocks. He was the mentor and inspiration of a whole generation of wine-makers.

Another outstanding Director has been Don Antonio Larrea Redondo, who retired in 1971 but is still active in wine circles. Scientist, scholar and historian, he is a much loved and respected figure, whose reputation as an oenologist extends far beyond the Rioja. The present lively and dynamic Director, Don Manuel Ruiz Hernández, has been responsible for a great deal of fundamental research into soils and climate, the characteristics of the different vine varieties, and the mechanism of wine-making and maturation. A selection of his research papers has been reprinted under the title of *Estudios sobre el vino de Rioja*.

Apart from basic research and co-operation with the growers and bodegas in resolving technical problems, the main work of the laboratory is the analysis and examination of Rioja wines so as to ensure that they comply with the requirements of the *Reglamento*. Samples of all wines destined for export must be lodged with the station, where they are tested for density, percentage of alcohol, acid and sugar content, etc. One of these tests is for *malvina*, a diglucosidic alkaloid found in wines made from hybrid American vines and banned by many importing countries, notably Germany, Switzerland and Austria. There are also systematic organoleptic tests, since it is a cardinal provision of the *Reglamento* that:

> Young wines, in common with those matured in oak, must possess organoleptic characteristics typical of the region, especially in regard to colour, aroma and flavour. Wines which, for any reason, do not in the judgement of the Consejo Regulador possess these qualities are not eligible for *Denominación de Origen* and will be disqualified in the prescribed form.

LABELLING

Wines exported to E.E.C. countries are labelled in accordance with the Community's rules for imports from 'Third Countries', and the labels of D.O. wines made in conformity with the *Reglamento* and entitled to the name 'Rioja' carry the following information:

Mandatory information	*Permitted information*
Geographical unit (Rioja)	Actual or total alcoholic strength
Country of origin (Spain)	Directions for serving
Name and address of bottler	Sweet/dry description
Name and address of importer	History
(if bottled in the Rioja)	Vine variety
Nominal volume	Vintage
	Superior quality description
Permitted information	Awards and medals
Red — white — rosé	Bottled on premises
Name and address of distributor	Name of vineyard
Citation ('Established in . . .', etc)	Quality control number

In addition to the main label, wines of superior quality carry a small back label with a description of type, i.e. '*vino de crianza*', '*reserva*' or '*gran reserva*' (see pp. 51-2). A typical approved label in the form is illustrated overleaf.

The content of the bottle is also subject to E.E.C. regulations: there are two standard sizes of bottle, a recommended one of 75 cl and a permitted one of 70 cl. The older established bodegas tend to use the larger size, and

Label in
authorized
E.E.C. form

Vintage — **VINTAGE 1971** | PRODUCE OF SPAIN — *Country of origin*

VINOS   FINOS

Name of producer — ESTATE BOTTLED BY — *Bottled on premises*

R. López de Heredia Viña Tondonia, S.A.

ESTABLISHED 1877

Guarantee of origin — REGULADOR RIOJA DENOMINACIÓN R E 333 LO — *Citation*

VIÑEDOS Y BODEGAS EN
HARO (RIOJA ALTA) — *Geographical unit*

TONDONIA
Rioja Fine Red — *Brand name* / *Superior quality descript*

Alcoholic strength — ALCOHOL 11,5°/₀ BY VOLUME   NOMINAL CONT. 70 CL. — *Nominal volume*
IMPORTED BY:
Importer — ROY GUNN WINES - 40 STATION AVE - COVENTRY

the newer, the smaller — but it is, in any case, marked on the label.

Labels used for the domestic market often describe the age of the wine in traditional fashion as 3° año, 5° año etc (see p. 50) referring to its age before bottling, rather than by stating a vintage year.

The words and phrases most commonly found on labels are as follows:

Añejo, añejado por	Old, aged by
Bodega	The concern which has made and/or shipped and sold the wine. Without further qualification it normally means that the bodega has made and shipped the wine.
Brut, brut natur	Dry, extra-dry, used only of sparkling wines.
Cepa	Literally, a 'vine'. Its use on labels is not precise, though the word is sometimes coupled with the name of a grape.
Cosecha	Vintage, e.g. Cosecha 1976
Criado por	Matured by
Denominación de Origen	The guarantee of the Consejo Regulador, printed on the label or back label in the form of a small facsimile stamp.
Elaborado por	Blended and, in the case of a mature wine, aged by
Embotellado por	Bottled by
Gran reserva	Mature wine of the best quality, aged in the case of *tinto* and *clarete*, for at least two years in oak cask and three in bottle.
Reserva	Mature wine of good quality, aged, in the case of *tinto* and *clarete*, for at least three years between oak cask and bottle, of which at least one must be in cask.
Sangría	Red wine containing citrus juice and aerated mineral water.
Vendimia	Vintage, e.g. Vendimia 1976
Viña, viñedo	Vineyard. Their use, coupled with the name of a vineyard, is not precise, but usually implies that the wine is made with at least a proportion of fruit from the named vineyard.
Vino	Wine
abocado	semi-sweet
blanco	white
clarete	light red
dulce	sweet
espumoso	sparkling
rosado	rosé
seco	dry
tinto	full-bodied red
Vino de crianza	Used on the back label, this indicates that the wine has been aged in oak in accordance with the rules of the *Reglamento* (see p. 51).

4 Soils, Vines AND VINEYARDS

The wine-growing area of the Rioja comprises some 44,000 hectares, 33,000 in the province of La Rioja (until recently known as Logroño), 7000 in the province of Alava and 4000 in a narrow southern strip of the province of Navarra bordering the River Ebro. It extends for a distance of some 120 km along the Ebro valley from the rocky gorge of the Conchas de Haro, where the River enters the region, to just east of the town of Alfaro in the east, and is bounded by mountains on both sides: the Sierra Cantábrica to the north and the great wooded massif of the Sierra de la Demanda to the south. The maximum width, between Anguciana in the Rioja Alta and Barriobusto in the Rioja Alavesa, is 50 km; and the vineyards are planted mainly along the valleys of the Ebro and its tributaries (the Oja, from which the region takes its name, and the Tirón, Najerilla, Iruega, Leza, Cidacos and Alhama), and on the lower slopes of the hills.

The altitude drops steadily from west to east, and the area is sheltered from cold north winds by the Sierra Cantábrica, and from parching south winds and the extremes of a continental climate by the serried ridges of the Sierra de la Demanda. In the hilly western sub-regions of the Rioja Alta and Rioja Alavesa, which produce the finest wines, the climate is Atlantic in type, with a certain amount of frost and snow in winter; mild, wet springs; short, hot summers and long, warm autumns. It is these favourable climatic conditions, in combination with the nature of the soils and quality of the vines, which account for the excellence of the wines.

The Rioja Baja to the east, designated as semi-arid by the Consejo Regulador, is generally sunnier and drier, with little or no snow in winter, and produces wines more of the Mediterranean type, robust and high in alcohol.

Geography and climatic conditions in the Rioja are summarized in the table:

Towns (west to east)	Height (metres)	Average annual temperature (°C)	Average annual rainfall (mm)
Haro	479	12.7	522
Nájera	435	9.8	508
Fuenmayor		13.2	438
Logroño	384	13.0	381
Sartaguda		13.8	387
Calahorra	350	13.4	343
Alfaro	301	14.4	284

THE SUB-REGIONS

It is customary to describe the wines in terms of the sub-regions. In general, those from the Rioja Alta contain more acid than the wines made from grapes grown with a southerly exposure in the Rioja Alavesa to the north of the Ebro; they tend to be fresher and brisker and to repay long ageing, while the wines from the Rioja Alavesa are softer and very fruity, and age more rapidly. Those from the Rioja Baja, made mainly from the black Garnacho, are fuller-bodied, higher in alcohol and less delicate than the wines from the other two sub-regions and are often sold for everyday drinking or blending.

The actual situation is a good deal more complicated. The Rioja was delimited on ecological grounds; but the division between the Rioja Alta and the Rioja Alavesa was made for administrative and political reasons (see p. 46), the Rioja Alavesa comprising the part of the region within the Province of Alava. It is clearly an anomaly that the Rioja Alta includes an enclave north of the Ebro, centring on Abalos, which geologically and climatically is of a piece with the Rioja Alavesa. Hard and fast distinctions between the wines are further blurred by the widespread blending of wines from the different sub-regions by the commercial bodegas and because they use different grape varieties in very different proportions.

In a recent book, *Manual de los vinos de Rioja* (Madrid, 1982), José Peñin poses the question: what is a classical Rioja? 'Is it the traditional Tondonia of Don Rafael López de Heredia made with the Graciano grape?

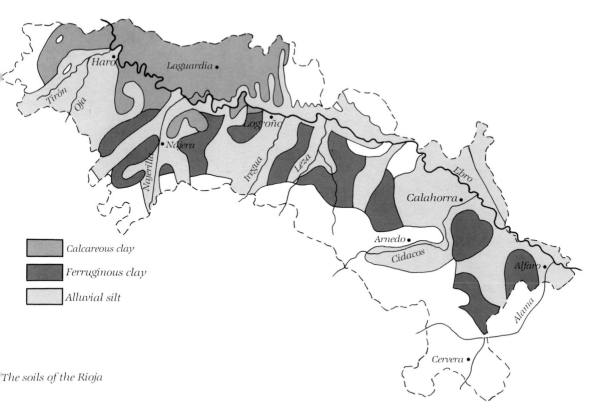

The soils of the Rioja

Is it CUNE with its delicate flavour of Tempranillo and Viura, or again the wine from Ramón Bilbao, copper-coloured and tasting of Garnacho?' He reaches the somewhat baffled conclusion that the one thing which distinguishes Rioja from other Spanish wines is its oaky nose and flavour.

Oenologists, such as Antonio Larrea and Manuel Ruiz Hernández have for some time considered that the most satisfactory method of classifying the wines is not simply according to sub-region, but on the basis of more detailed considerations of soils and ampelography.

SOILS

Differences in the types of soil is at once visible in driving around the Rioja: in the Rioja Alavesa it is usually a pale yellow ochre, and in the other sub-regions, often a deep orange-red, denoting the presence of iron. The three basic types, whose occurrence is shown in the accompanying map, are calcareous clay, ferruginous clay, alluvial silt.

The ferruginous clay and silt, carried down by the Ebro and its tributaries, usually lie above an underlying layer of calcareous clay, and the deposits of ferruginous clay often occur on hilly ground dividing the soils of the other two types.

The light-coloured calcareous soil of the first type, generally considered to be the most suitable for viticulture, is made up of sandstone, limestone, marl and clay, and contains up to 40 to 45 per cent of calcium carbonate and is therefore of low acidity. It occurs throughout the Rioja Alavesa and also in the Rioja Alta around Villalba, Haro, Galbárruli, Sajazarra, Fonzalechem, Cuzcurrita, Tirgo, Briones, Gimileo, Ollauri, San Asensio, Cenicero and Fuenmayor. The wines made from vines grown on these soils are deep in colour, high in glycerine and extract, resistant to pathological attack, but somewhat low in acid and are largely those which have established the high reputation of Rioja.

The most important alluvial zones lie around Tiron-Oja and Glera in the far west of the Rioja Alta, around Tuerto and Nájera to the south of the sub-region, and are widespread in the river basins of the Rioja Baja. The wines are low in extract and minerals, prone to oxidation and changes of colour, and typically high in alcohol and acidity. This type of soil is the least suitable for viticulture, though well-adapted for growing cereals, vegetables and potatoes.

The ferruginous clays, with their high content of iron salts and a calcium carbonate content of 10 to 25 per cent are intermediate in quality between the other two types and are most prevalent in the Rioja Baja, with further scattered areas in the Rioja Alta. In general, Sr Ruiz Hernández considers that calcareous clay is the best for red wines, ferruginous clay for *claretes* and rosés, and alluvial silt for white wines.

The wines might be typified as follows:

Rioja Alavesa

Red wines made principally from the Tempranillo with smaller amounts of white Viura and other varieties. Aromatic, fruity, deep in colour, but somewhat low in acid and quick to mature, they are among the best from the whole area.

Haro

Made from differing proportions of all the grapes authorized by the Consejo Regulador, grown both on calcareous and alluvial soils, the wines are ruby-coloured and fresh, with less nose than those from the Rioja Alavesa, but higher in acidity and longer-lasting.

San Asensio

Perched on a hilltop between Haro and Cenicero, San Asensio lies at the centre of an area of calcareous clay and makes fresh *claretes* and rosés with good acid balance from Garnacho and Viura grapes.

Cenicero-Fuenmayor

Situated in another area of calcareous clay, these townships in the Rioja Alta make some of the very best Riojas, with a high proportion of Tempranillo. More fully bodied than the wines from Haro, they are more acidic than those from the Rioja Alavesa and age better.

Rioja Baja

This is the one sub-region to be demarcated solely in accordance with soil and climate. With its arid climate and soil composed either of ferruginous clay or alluvial silt, it makes wines of the Mediterranean type, high in alcohol and of low acidity. The tendency of its red wines to oxidise is reinforced by an almost exclusive use of red Garnacho.

Low-growing vines near Labastida, with the Sierra Cantábrica in the background

Cuzcurrita

One of the highest, wettest and most westerly areas of the Rioja Alta, with alluvial and calcareous soils, Cuzcurrita makes wines more acidic and tannic than most, which repay long ageing.

CLIMATE

Climatic conditions have already been summarized (pp. 59-60). In general, the higher rainfall and cooler temperatures of the Rioja Alta and Rioja Alavesa give rise to wines containing more acid and less alcohol (normally around 12 per cent by volume) than those from the hotter and drier Rioja Baja, where the wines are of the Mediterranean type and the high sugar content of the grapes results in low acidity and alcohol content often in excess of 13 per cent by volume.

Because of the southerly aspect of the vineyards on the slopes of the Sierra Cantábrica in the Rioja Alavesa, the grapes receive more sunshine

*The Sierra
Cantábrica
above
Laguardia*

*Vineyards in the
Rioja Alavesa,
with the Sierra
Cantábrica in
the background*

*Vineyards near
Villabuena
in the
Rioja Alavesa
at harvest time*

and yield musts with rather more alcohol and less acid than those from the Rioja Alta. There are also differences in microclimate within the sub-regions, Nájera and Cuzcurrita, for example, in the Rioja Alta being markedly less sunny than Haro or Cenicero; and this is reflected in the character of the musts.

There are, of course, marked variations in the weather from one year to another, though these are perhaps somewhat less than in Bordeaux, so that vintages tend to be more consistent.

By and large, climatic conditions leading to a satisfactory harvest and good quality are well-known: plenty of rain in the spring to ensure vegetative growth, a sunny summer, a little rain later to swell the fruit and dry weather at harvest time. Conversely, hailstorms in the late spring and early summer damage the buds and flowers; persistent rain during the summer may well lead to rot and mildew. This was the case in 1971, when above-average rainfall resulted in the onset of mildew and the loss of 65 per cent of the crop in some areas. 1972 was another wet and disastrous year; in 1977, heavy rainfall held back the ripening of the grapes and was followed by a damp autumn giving rise to microbial infections; while in 1979, torrential rain at harvest time diluted the musts and weakened the wine.

Sr Ruiz Hernández has published a series of papers (*Estudios sobre el vino de Rioja*) investigating the less apparent influences of climatic conditions on the quality of the wines. One conclusion is that a most important factor is the mean daily temperature during the six weeks preceding the harvest. A higher than average temperature does not necessarily lead to good quality, but does militate in favour of the following year's harvest, since it helps the plant to store nutriment during the winter.

Even more significant than absolute temperature at this period is the temperature gradient (i.e. the difference between maximum daytime and minimum night-time temperature) during the ten days before picking. A high temperature gradient promotes increased amounts of enzymatic oxidases in the musts, so impeding satisfactory ageing and rendering the wine liable to premature oxidative breakdown; and a high proportion of a grape like the Garnacho, whose musts are particularly prone to oxidation, catalyzes the process. Oddly enough, relative humidity and rainfall during the run-up to the harvest have little influence on the all-important redox potentials of musts made with sound grapes.

Such studies perhaps explain why, with lower than average temperatures at harvest time, but less than average variations of night-time and daytime temperatures, the 1970 vintage turned out to be the best of its decade.

Because of adverse weather conditions, there was a run of low crops

he tree-lined ourse of the River Ebro, rom the Castle of San Vicente

during the latter 1970s, which seriously depleted the reserves of the large bodegas and led to higher prices. Subsequent years saw much larger harvests, but of late, much of Spain has been afflicted by near drought conditions, which have affected the production, if not the quality of the wine.

Average annual production in the Rioja over the last ten years stands at 110 million litres; individual figures for recent years follow:

Vintage	Yield (millions of litres)	Quality
1970	114	Excellent
1971	55	Poor
1972	99	Very poor
1973	128	Good
1974	131	Average
1975	84	Good
1976	93	Good
1977	65	Very poor
1978	81	Very good
1979	140	Average
1980	125	Good
1981	130	Very good
1982	105	Excellent
1983	95	Good

VINE VARIETIES

In the past, the grapes of more than a dozen different varieties of vine have been used for making Rioja wines, but of these the Consejo Regulador now authorizes only seven for wines qualifying for *Denominación de Origen*. These are:

Black grapes	*White grapes*
Tempranillo	Viura
Garnacho	Malvasía
Mazuelo	Garnacho blanco
Graciano	

It is thought that, of these seven varieties, the Tempranillo, Mazuelo and Graciano are native to the region; and that the Garnachos were introduced centuries ago from Aragón, and the Malvasía from Greece.

It is often stated that the autoctonous black Tempranillo is the most widespread, but the fact is that up to 1935, 6500 hectares of vineyards in the Rioja were planted with the black Garnacho, as against 3000 with Tempranillo. Until 1965, more Garnacho than Tempranillo was being planted; and only after 1970 has the proportion of Tempranillo and the white Viura been increased at its expense. The present position is that 44 per cent of the vineyards are planted with Garnacho, 22 per cent with Tempranillo and 15 per cent with Viura, the balance being made up by other varieties.

The history and characteristics of the different varieties have been described in a booklet *Vides de la Rioja*, published by the Ministry of Agriculture and originally compiled by Don Victor Cruz Manso de Zuñiga. The third edition of 1978 has been updated by Don Antonio Larrea.

Tempranillo

Although it is generally accepted that the Tempranillo is a native of the Rioja, there are those who hold that it was originally introduced by monks from the monasteries of Clury or Cîteaux at the time of the mediaeval pilgrimage to Santiago de Compostela, in the form of the Pinot noir or Cabernet franc. Certain it is that it is widely-grown in other parts of Spain under different names to produce their best red wines. So, in Catalonia it is known as the Ull de Llebre, in Valdepeñas as the Cencibel, in the Ribera del Duero as the Tinto fino, and in Arganda as the Tinto Madrid. Such is its quality that experiments are currently under way to acclimatize it in California and Australia.

The Tempranillo is the grape *par excellence* of the Rioja Alavesa; it also flourishes in the calcareous clay of various area of the Rioja Alta, although the character of the musts is somewhat different as between, say, Cenicero and Labastida, and different again from those produced outside the Rioja, where its wines do not possess quite the same fragrance, balance or delicacy.

Unlike the Garnacho, which thrives in the arid conditions of the Rioja Baja, it grows best in the cooler and more humid western areas of the Rioja and, like the Pinot noir from which it is sometimes supposedly derived, is resistant to cold. Although generally robust, the vines are susceptible to *oidium* and mildew, and it is so-called (*tempranillo*, 'early') because its grapes ripen in the latter part of September, about a fortnight before the Garnacho. Thick-skinned and intensely black, their musts are less sweet than those of the Garnacho, producing fragrant and fruity wines of from 10.5° to 13.5° with good acid balance.

One of the great virtues of the Tempranillo is that its musts are low in oxidases, so permitting extended ageing.

Garnacho tinto

The Garnacho, easy to cultivate and with good yield, is the grape most widely grown in the Rioja and Spain as a whole. In the Rioja Baja it is grown to the exclusion of most other varieties, but there are also extensive plantations around San Asensio and Mormejilla in the Rioja Alta, where it gives rise to lighter and more delicate wines. It is known in other parts of Spain as the Tinto aragonés and Alicante; in France as the Grenache of the Rhône Valley; and in Italy as the Granaccia or Uva di Spagna.

It grows well in stony and clay soils and in a dry, hot environment. The vines, vigorous and erect, are subject to attack by mildew, but resistant to *oidium*. The grapes, round, black and thick-skinned, ripen in early October; and the flesh is colourless or greenish. The musts yield wines fruity when young, though somewhat hard because of the amount of tartaric acid and high in alcohol (up to 15°-16°). In poor years these are often blended with others to lend strength and body. They do not possess great depth of colour, and the Garnacho is sometimes picked early in the Rioja Alta to make *claretes* and rosés.

The musts, particularly those made with ripe grapes from the Rioja Baja, oxidise very easily; and the colour of a Garnacho wine is not a reliable indication of age, as it may fairly soon turn to brick-red or orange.

Graciano

Found in the oldest vineyards of the Rioja and not encountered abroad or in other parts of Spain, the Graciano is thought to be a native of the region.

It grows best in the same conditions as the Tempranillo, but in less compacted soils. With its thin shoots, it is nevertheless highly resistant to diseases, and it is one of the easiest varieties to identify in a vineyard, since its leaves turn first to a brilliant yellow, then to tones of russet and red, and are the last to fall.

The grapes ripen in early October and are intensely black, with thin skins and large round pips. The musts contain ony 10° to 12° of alcohol, but confer great freshness, fragrance and flavour on the wines. Although the celebrated oenologist Juan Marcilla considered that the Graciano was responsible for the best and most typical Riojan nose, even in the Rioja Alta it is being grown in decreasing amount, since it is less fertile than the other varieties and more difficult to cultivate.

Mazuelo

Possibly the same variety as the Crujillon or Carignanne of Hérault, the Mazuelo is found in the oldest vineyards of the Rioja and is thought to be a native of the region or of neighbouring Navarra. It grows mainly in the Rioja Alta and Rioja Baja in areas of calcareous clay.

Its growth cycle is similar to that of the Garnacho, but its cultivation has decreased because of its susceptibility to *oidium*. Its grapes, which ripen in early October, are large, of an intense black with firm flesh. The musts are deep in colour, without much aroma, and astringent to the taste because of a high tannin content. They are also highly resistant to oxidation and for this reason are often blended with wines destined for long maturation.

The vineyards of the Marqués de Murrieta near Logroño

Viura

The white Viura was introduced to the Rioja from Aragón in 1850 and is variously known in other regions of Spain as the Alcañon and Alcañol, and in Catalonia as the Macabeo. It is now the most widespread of the white grapes in the Rioja and is the white variety preferred by the Consejo Regulador.

Especially in calcareous clay, the vine fruits abundantly, ripening during the first fortnight in October and yielding musts with good acid balance and resistance to oxidation. The wines are both fragrant and intensly fruity, and it is the variety most used (sometimes 100 per cent) for the new-style 'cold fermented' white wines. In the Rioja Alavesa some 10 per cent of the must is often added to red Tempranillo wines to improve the balance, fragrance and flavour.

Malvasía

The Malvasía must be one of the most widely-distributed of white grapes. A native of Asia Minor, it was first introduced to Spain by Greek settlers in Catalonia and is variously known in different parts of the country as Blanquirroja, Tobía and Blanca-roja, and is found in the oldest vineyards of the Rioja Alta. In the form of Malmsey, a corruption of the original Greek 'Monemvasia', it has also given its name to one of the most famous Madeiras, and is additionally grown in the Canary Islands.

It grows best in a dry environment and on high ground, and the vines are vigorous and large-leaved, but somewhat prone to mildew. The grapes ripen in early October, with a marked rise in sugar content during the last days on the vine, and yield large amounts of a bitter-sweet golden yellow must. The wines are fragrant and unctuous. It is often used for white wines in conjunction with the Viura, or on its own for the traditional white Riojas with long maturation in cask, but the musts are easily oxidizable and care must be taken to avoid early maderization.

Garnacho blanco

Introduced to the Rioja from Aragón, the Garnacho blanco is not so much used as the other varieties approved by the Consejo Regulador, but is prolific and easily cultivated on most types of soil, and also more resistant to disease than the other varieties of white grape. The musts are fresh and high in alcohol, though low in acid.

Other vine varieties, of less importance, but traditionally grown in the Rioja and still used by the smaller producers in admixture with the approved varieties, are:

Calagrano

This white grape, widely grown in the area of Cuzcurrita in the far south-west of the Rioja Alta is also known as the Navés and Cazagal and appears to be identical with the Cayetana, much cultivated in the Extremadura, bordering Portugal.

A prolific producer, its musts are tart and of low alcoholic degree, containing little sugar; but it has its followers, who maintain that when the grapes are fully ripe, the wines are delicate and fragrant.

Maturana blanca

A white grape, with certain similarities to the Merlot from Bordeaux, which has been grown for centuries in the Rioja, but is now increasingly little-used. Its musts are bitter-sweet and agreeable, with high sugar content but little acidity.

Maturana tinta

Like the white variety, the black is thought to be related to the Merlot and has long been grown in the Rioja, but is no longer being planted.

Miguel del Arco

Also known as the Arcos and Miguelete, this black grape is grown in Navarra, Aragón and Valencia, as well as in the Rioja. It flourishes in the dry soils and environment of the Rioja Baja and is resistant to mildew, producing musts without much colour and low in alcohol.

Monastrel

The black Monastrel, also known as the Valcarcelía, Monastel, Moraster, Ministrel, Negralejo and Mechín, is grown in the Rioja Baja and Navarra, but produces the best wine in Catalonia.

Moscatel

Grown only to a very limited extent in the Rioja, this is the familiar Muscat, employed to such advantage in making sweet wines in Málaga, the Levante, Jerez and overseas.

Turruntés

A classic black grape, long native in the Rioja, the Turruntés gave birth to the rhyme:

Turruntés,
Ni lo comas ni lo des,
Que para buen vino es.

Don't eat or give Turruntés
It is good only for wine.

This notwithstanding, the Turruntés is now not much cultivated, and its musts, though abundant, fresh and high in alcohol, are markedly acid, like those of the Calagraño.

The proportions in which the different grape varieties are used in making the red wines differ from one sub-region to another and from bodega to bodega (for details, see Chapter 7). As Sr Larrea once wrote:

> A pure Garnacho wine would easily become characterless and too high in alcohol content to accompany a good meal. A Tempranillo alone would tend to be 'soft' — short-lived because of insufficient acidity — and slightly rough. A Graciano would be delicious but too scarce for the market and too low in alcohol, and a Mazuelo would be excessively high in both colour and tannin.

A typical blend in the Rioja Alta might be 60 per cent Tempranillo, 25 per cent Garnacho and 15 per cent Graciano and Mazuelo. In the Rioja Alavesa it is customary to use 90 per cent or more of Tempranillo, with the addition of a little white Viura, while the red wines from the Rioja Baja contain a very high proportion of Garnacho tinto.

The white wines, especially those of the new-style, 'cold fermented' type, are increasingly made with 100 per cent Viura, but often contain amounts of Malvasía or Garnacho blanco.

The best of the rosés are made from the black Garnacho, especially that grown in the Rioja Alta, picked young and left only briefly in contact with the skins to extract a little colour.

CULTIVATION

The typical vineyards in the Rioja Alta and Rioja Alavesa are small and interspersed with fields of potatoes, vegetables and wheat. The average size is only 4.4 hectares, and this has resulted from the splitting up of land between the sons on the death of their father. Because of the small size, one tradition which still survives is for two neighbours to share the labour of cultivation and also the equipment and a small bodega, dividing the

Modern vineyard belonging to Bodegas Berberana

wine according to the amount of grapes produced on each of the plots. Another system, somewhat similar to the *Rabassa Morta* of Catalonia, is the *aparcería*, whereby the farmer is leased the vineyard in return for his labour and makes over half of the wine to the proprietor.

Since the boom of the late nineteenth century, the larger commercial bodegas have bought up land and some, like Riscal, Murrieta, López de Heredia and La Rioja Alta, may grow as much as 40 per cent of their grapes, naming their wines after vineyards such as Tondonia or Zaco, but buying the rest of the fruit from independent farmers. In this case the bodega regularly supervises the vineyards of its suppliers and may, if the fruit is below standard, pay an agreed minimum and allow them to sell it elsewhere.

The huge new bodegas constructed during the 1970s tend to buy grapes or wine from the co-operatives or in the open market, though a few, like Berberana and Domecq, have invested heavily in new plantations — sometimes running into financial difficulties in the course of this expensive exercise. Pedro Domecq owns 571 hectares in the best part of the Rioja Alavesa, while Berberana launched on an ambitious project of developing some 900 hectares at Monte Yerga, a carefully chosen area in the Rioja Baja.

In the Rioja Baja, with its rolling hills and flatter terrain, vineyards tend to be larger and often adjoin vast fields of peppers and asparagus.

When *phylloxera* first broke out in 1899 in the vineyards of Sajazarra in the Rioja Alta, the first attempt to control it was by injecting chemicals such as carbon disulphide into the ground — and perhaps it is more than mere suggestion when one seems to detect traces on the palate in some of the very old wines from the cellars of Paternina in Ollauri. The epidemic spread rapidly through the whole region. By 1901 production had decreased by some 86 per cent and thousands of families were ruined and had emigrated. However, the attack was brought under fairly rapid control by the Estación Enologica (see p. 53) by the now familiar method of grafting shoots of the native varieties of *Vitis vinifera* on to American stocks resistant to the ravages of the voracious aphid, which blights the vines by sucking the substance from their roots.

As elsewhere in Europe, and generally, grafting is now standard practice; and the root stocks most commonly employed are those of the American *Vitis riparia* or *Vitis rupestris*, or the *Berlandieri* and its hybrids. Grafting, which involves the careful splicing of the grape-producing vine into the resistant root stock, may be carried out in the field or by bench-grafting, and many concerns prefer to buy ready-grafted vines from a nursery.

The vines, as is still the case in many of the smaller and older vineyards, were formerly planted with different varieties in the proportions used in making the wine. A disadvantage of this system is that the different varieties do not ripen at the same time, so that if they are picked simultaneously, the Tempranillo will be ripe or over-ripe, while the Garnacho is not fully mature. The *Reglamento* (see pp. 47-53) now provides that in new vineyards the different varieties must be planted apart, so allowing for picking at the optimum time; blending of the musts may then, if necessary, be carried out after fermentation.

In the older vineyards, random replacement of the vines at the end of their useful life (of up to fifty or sixty years, when the must is small in amount, but often of excellent quality), had led to complete disarray. This did not matter when all the operations of tillage and viticulture were carried out by hand. Later practice was to plant the vines in soldierly rows two *varas* (or 1.74 m) apart, with about 1.5 m between the individual plants in a row. With the increasing use of tractor-drawn implements (though mechanized harvesting has not yet been employed in the Rioja), the most modern vineyards are being planted with 3 m between the rows and 1 m between the stocks, at a density of about 3,330 plants per hectare.

Conventional wisdom, embodied in the *Reglamento*, is that the best results are obtained by growing the vines low and pruning them *en vaso* ('goblet-shaped'). In this method the vine is left with three *brazos* or main stems, each bearing two *pulgares* or grafted shoots producing two *racimos* or bunches of grapes, i.e. twelve in all.

To those used to the leafy vineyards of Bordeaux, with the vines growing luxuriantly along wires supported by stakes, the low, unsupported vines of the Rioja present a somewhat stunted appearance. The Consejo Regulador has, however relented to the extent of allowing a firm like Pedro Domecq to experiment with vines planted in Bordeaux fashion and pruned by the Guyot method, making for higher yield. The results have been encouraging, and quality appears to be unaffected.

The work of tending a vineyard is ceaseless and continues all through the year. In the small vineyards it is still carried out by hand or with a plough drawn by a horse or mule, the animal sometimes being shared by adjacent small proprietors. The larger concerns make increasing use of tractors and mechanized aids.

The pruning of the oldest vines begins in the autumn, after the harvest:

> *Si la viña vieja quieres volver, moza,*
> *pódala con hoja.*

> If you want old vines to flourish, lass,
> prune them while still in leaf.

Pruning knives

However, it is more usual to begin pruning in January, and another refrain runs:

> *Quien cava en enero y poda en febrero*
> *tendrá buen año uvero.*

> He who digs in January and prunes in February
> will have a good year in the vineyards.

The object of pruning is to strengthen the plant and to ensure that during the growing season the sap goes to producing grapes, and not un-

wanted foliage, which further shades the berries and hinders their ripening. In the large vineyards the bulk of the vegetative shoots or *sarmientos* are cut mechanically—and often used for the grilling of the small lamb chops, a gastronomic speciality of the region (see p. 156). More refined pruning, undertaken to limit the number of grape-bearing shoots, is carried out by hand with a curved knife, the *podón*, or with secateurs.

The work of digging around the roots of the vine, so as to aerate the soil, and of mounding it around the stocks so as to collect the winter rains, known as *cavalta*, proceeds throughout the winter, beginning in December or January. Nowadays, this is done with tractors by deep ploughing, but in the past a host of *cavadores* descended on the Rioja from Galicia and the mountains of the north, spending up to five months in the area. A day's work or '*obrero*' was set at the digging of two hundred vines; and an eighteenth-century document refers to 'the huge consumption of vegetables [by the labourers], since the season lasts for one hundred and forty days and they feed three times a day, eating only *ollas* (hot-pots) of beans.'

Lighter tillage of the soil to remove weeds is carried out from May onwards.

Farmyard manure or, alternatively, *orujo*—the pips and skins remaining from wine-making — is applied every three or four years during the winter, and inorganic calciums and super-phosphates are used every year.

The only two diseases to present much of a problem in the Rioja are mildew and *oidium*. Mildew (*plasmopera viticola*) was of American origin and was first observed in the Rioja in 1834. It is combatted by repeated spraying with copper sulphate during the growing season from May onwards. *Oidium*, a fungal disease of the leaves which spread from England in 1845 (see p. 34) is treated by powdering the leaves with sulphur. The vines are also liable to attack by a variety of insect pests, notably the *piral* (*sparganotis pilleriana*), formerly dealt with by stripping the stocks and lighting bonfires in the vineyards, so attracting and incinerating the butterflies. Pests such as these may nowadays be eliminated a great deal more effectively with modern insecticides.

THE WINE HARVEST

Grape-picking in the Rioja starts traditionally on October 10th, rather after the week-long Fiesta de San Mateo in Logroño beginning on September 21st. In fact, harvesting of the earlier-ripening Tempranillo grapes begins about a fortnight before.

*ocal growers
xhibit their
ines during
he harvest
stival in
enicero*

La Virgen de
los Parrales
(the vines)

Vº Rº DE LA MILAGROSA IMAGEN DE NRA. SEÑORA DE LOS PARRALES.
Que fue aparecida entre vnas Parras extramuros dela Villa d Bañes d Riotouia
Estan concedidas 460 dias de Indulujencias por varios Señores Arzobispos y Obispos
Rezando una Salbe delante de esta Sta Imagen y sus Estampas.
Adeboçion de un deboto Nral de dha. Villa,
y á sus Expensas.

Palomino. f.

Logroño, the capital of the recently re-named Province of La Rioja, is at its liveliest during the festival, the crowded cafés putting out trestle tables in the narrow alleys leading down to the Ebro, a uniformed band parading the streets, and the crowds converging late at night on the wide Paseo del Espolón, where celebrations finish with spectacular firework displays.

Towns and villages up and down the Rioja celebrate the harvest, the people often carrying a statue of their patron saint through the streets and draping it with grapes. The patroness of the Rioja as a whole is the Virgin of Valvanera, whose eleventh-century effigy is preserved in the Monastery of Valvanera (see p. 28), high above the wooded Najerilla valley in the Sierra de la Demanda. A traditional rhyme runs:

> *María de Valvanera,*
> *Presta color a las vides*
> *Y nunca jamás me olvides*
> *Ni aun después de que me muera.*

> María de Valvanera,
> Lend heat to the vines
> And never forget me
> Even after I die.

Haro celebrates its most famous festival, 'La Batalla del Vino', when crowds converge on the main square and squirt all and sundry with wine from leathern *botas*, not at harvest time, but in July. It is, however, of recent origin and appears to have been modelled on similar juncketings at the village of Santa Ana in the Rioja Baja, discontinued some time ago because of the riotous scenes with which it inevitably ended!

As to the more serious business of picking the grapes, whole families arrive from other rural districts of northern Spain, either camping out or lodging in the barrack-like hostels provided by some of the bodegas, such as Riscal. The itinerant band of harvesters are known as *cuadrillas forasteras* and are in charge of a veteran picker, the *mayoral*. They may either contract their services '*a seco*' (without food) or '*a mojado*', when a meal or meals are provided.

When the grapes are destined for *vino corriente*, vine is completely stripped of grapes, ripe or unripe. The fruit used for fine Riojas is gathered with care, first the grapes close to the stock and with a southerly aspect, and then those which require more ripening, at the ends of the branches and with a northerly exposure. The pickers use either a curved knife, or *corquete*, or secateurs, and the small farmers, as they have done for centuries,

*A plastic-draped
trailer used
for transporting
the grapes to
the bodega*

first pick the grapes into a wicker basket, then tipping them into wooden *comportones*, holding some 80 to 120 kg, for transport to the bodega. The traditional mule-cart with its two high wheels has largely been replaced by tractor-drawn trailers of every size and shape.

To bruise the grapes as little as possible, and to avoid premature fermentation, the large bodegas are now picking the fruit into plastic boxes (like those used in Jerez) and holding some 17 kg. The contents are transferred to large, plastic-draped trailers, and the load is driven straight to the bodega, weighed and checked for sugar content, then tipped into a hopper and fed into the crusher. It may therefore reach the fermentation vat within quarter-of-an-hour of being picked. During peak times at a large bodega, like that of the Marqués de Riscal, there are queues of grape-laden trailers, both those belonging to the firm and to independent growers, waiting their turn at the reception bay; but it is a matter of pride that all the fruit should begin fermentation on the day that it is picked and work continues long after dark.

Thousands of small growers take their fruit to be vinified at the local co-operative; and here the procedure is similar. The trailer first passes to a weighing bridge, a sampler sucks out grapes and automatically records the sugar content, and the fruit is then conveyed by a *tolvo* (or Archimedean screw) to the crusher, the *socio* being paid on the basis of weight and sugar content.

5 MAKING AND MATURING RIOJA

The Rioja makes a great deal more red wine than white or rosé, average annual production (prior to a run of disappointing harvests in the 1970s) amounting to 100 million litres of *tinto*, 20 million litres of *blanco* and 20 million litres of *rosado*.

VINIFICATION OF RED WINES

There are two methods of vinifying the red wines: the traditional, used for centuries by the *cosecheros* or small producers, and the Bordeaux method, first introduced on a commercial scale at the bodegas of the Marqués de Riscal and Marqués de Murrieta (see pp. 33-36), and now universally employed by the large bodegas. Nevertheless, of the 2646 bodegas in the region, more than 2100 still use the old method. In fact, some of the co-operatives, like that of San Vincente de la Sonsierra, having installed modern plant, have actually reverted to the old *lagos* since their customers, often in the Basque country and the north, insisted on the fat, fleshy wines in the traditional style.

The historic method has already been described (see p. 35). Since the grapes are not crushed but remain whole, submerged in the must emerging from such as are broken, it is an intracellular fermentation and largely anaerobic, taking place under a blanket of carbon dioxide. It therefore resembles the *macération carbonique* used for making Beaujolais Nouveau, and the wines are somewhat similar in character, fresh and fruit, ready

*Sorting
the grapes*

for drinking within two months of fermentation, but low both in malic and tartaric acids and unsuitable for ageing for more than two years.

Red Rioja as made by the commercial bodegas for consumption in Spain, or shipment abroad is radically different in that it is fermented in contact with air.

On arrival at the bodega, the grapes are weighed and the sugar content measured. Mixed according to variety in the correct proportions, they are then fed into a hopper and conveyed by means of an Archimedean screw to a crusher, which at the same time removes and rejects the stalks, which would otherwise make the wine excessively tannic. Earlier ripening varieties, such as the Tempranillo, may be fermented separately, and in this case the musts will be blended at a later stage. A little sulphur, usually in the form of potassium metabisulphite, is added to inactivate undesirable yeasts, such as *Torúla*, *Torulaspora* and *Kloechera apiculata*, and the must, containing the skins and pips, but not the stalks, is pumped into the fermentation vats, filled four-fifths full to allow for the frothing of the wine and to avoid its overflowing.

In the older and more traditional bodegas, such as López de Heredia and La Rioja Alta, the vats, known as *tinas*, are made of American oak. Riscal and Murrieta, as also most of the co-operatives, use concrete vats coated with tartrate or a vitrified epoxy resin; and in the new generation of bodegas the trend is towards large stainless-steel tanks of up to 50,000 litres capacity. These are completely hygienic and easy to clean, and are either double-jacketed, allowing for the circulation of refrigerant, or may be cooled by running water over the outside. This makes possible slower fermentation of the wine at temperatures of 20°C to 25°C, so conserving fruitiness and flavour.

Tumultuous fermentation, brought about by the action of the yeast *Saccharomyces cerevisiae*, present in the form of a bloom on the skins of the grapes, sets in almost at once with the breakdown of the grape sugar into alcohol and the vigorous evolution of carbon dioxide. The gas carries up the skins and solid matter to the surface of the liquid, and the *sombrero* or 'cap' is regularly broken up and submerged, either by rodding it with spiked or flanged poles known as *mecedores* or *basuqueadores*, or on a larger scale by a pump which redistributes the solids inside the vat or sprays the liquid on top of the 'cap'. Many of the modern bodegas have installed auto-matic fermentation tanks, working like a coffee percolator, in which there is continuous circulation of the must and submersion of the 'cap'.

In a wooden or concrete vat, vigorous fermentation normally takes place at between 28°C to 30°C and lasts for about three days; in a tem-perature-controlled steel vat it will last for considerably longer. In either case, the wine is left for another week or so, and then decanted off the solid matter at the bottom into a fresh vat, usually concrete or wooden in the older establishments. This leaves some 20 per cent of the wine at the bottom of the fermentation vat, mixed with skins and pips, from which it is freed by pressing. The older bodegas use upright hydraulic basket presses with slatted wooden sides, while the newer employ horizontal presses of the

Loading the residue from the fermentation vat into a basket press

type used for white wine (see page 88). The *vino de prensa* or press wine is dark and much richer in tannin than the *vino de yema*, first drawn off the fermentation vat, but a proportion may be added to it to achieve better balance and longer life.

The new wine is turbid and is left to settle out until December or January, when it is decanted afresh into another large vat. The traditional time for this in the Rioja was at the time of the first new moon in January. It seems that the phases of the moon may have some influence on wine-making, but modern practice is to carry out the operation in early December.

At this stage a slow secondary or malo-lactic fermentation brought about by naturally occurring bacteria sets in, resulting in the transformation

*ine running
ɔm the press
ɩo a storage
stern*

of harsh-tasting malic acid into the smoother lactic, with marked improvement in flavour. At the same time, the winter cold causes the precipitation of tartaric acid and solid matter, and the wine is again racked (or decanted) into fresh vats in April.

About June, the wine is racked into individual casks, the 225-litre *barricas* or *bordelesas*, to begin the second phase of maturation.

Claretes are vinified in the same fashion as the fuller-bodied *tintos*, except that the skins and pips are left in contact with the fermenting must for a shorter period, so that less of the tannins and colouring matter pass into the wine.

VINIFICATION OF WHITE WINES

The vinification of white wines is basically different from that of reds in that the grapes are first pressed, with or without the stalks, and fermented *en virgen*, i.e. apart from the stalks, skins and pips. In practice, there are several variations of this method.

The small growers (or *cosecheros*) press the grapes without separating the stalks and run the must into cement tanks to ferment. After settling out and racking, the wine is then aged in oak casks. Wines made in this way are a pronounced yellow in colour and often taste of little but oak, since the temperature of fermentation may rise to between 30°C and 35°C with consequent loss of fruit in the nose and flavour.

Without sophisticated equipment or temperature-controlled fermentation, the Cooperativa Vinícola de Labastida (see p. 144) makes one of the fruitiest and most delicate white wines of the region. The grapes are tipped into a large cement vat and left overnight. As with the luscious *lágrimas* of Málaga, juice emerges from the grapes without mechanical means as a result of pressure from the fruit at the top of the load. It is therefore a must obtained only from the pulp nearest the skins of the ripest grapes and is transferred to a separate vat for fermentation.

Procedure again varies in the large bodegas. It begins with the pressing of the grapes in a large horizontal press. This may work either by breaking up the grapes and squeezing out the must through the slatted sides by circular plates or, in the more modern Willmes type of German design, by the repeated expansion and deflation of a large rubber bag and the squeezing of the pulp against the sides of the press. Sophisticated versions of the continuous press are also employed – the disadvantage of the older being that they bruised the skins, stalks and pips, so incorporating bitter tannic elements into the must.

The must is allowed to settle out and may be cleared by centrifugation or by the addition of clarifying agents and is sterilized by light addition of sulphur dioxide. It is important that this should not be over-enthusiastic, since it is difficult to clear a wine of the pronounced taste of sulphur and of aldehydes, resulting from overdosage and chemical interaction. This is a common defect of many white wines.

Fermentation is slower in beginning than with red wines owing to the absence of the skins and the yeasts adhering to them and, especially for the new-style white wines, cultured yeasts are often added. Depending on the characteristics of the must, there may also be a small addition of citric or tartaric acid to achieve a satisfactory balance. Avoidance of unnecessary contact with air, and consequent oxidation, is particularly to be avoided.

In a rootedly traditional bodega, such as López de Heredia, fermentation is carried out in the traditional wooden vats, and the wines are then matured in oak *barricas* along the same lines as the reds – great care being taken to avoid unnecessary exposure to the atmosphere during the operations of racking. They are then aged in oak barrels for periods of up to twelve years;

Barricas *of*
maturing wine
in the cellars of
C.V.N.E.

*Modern steel
fermentation
tanks at
Bodegas
Berberana*

and as Hugh Johnson has remarked in his *Wine Companion* (Mitchell Beazley, 1983), 'Outstanding examples of these *reservas* remain pale lemon-yellow and keep an astonishing freshness, roundness and vigour beneath a great canopy of oak fragrance. They can be compared with the best old vintages of white Graves'.

In response to foreign demands for lighter, fragrant and fruitier white wines, the large bodegas are increasingly turning to 'cold fermentation' in stainless-steel tanks. This involves a very slow fermentation at temperatures between 14°C and 18°C for periods ranging from a month to six weeks. The grape most favoured for these wines, because of its resistance to oxidation and the light and agreeable bouquet and flavour of its musts, is the Viura. Wines of this type are aged in oak, if at all, only briefly. They are bottled early and should be drunk while young and fresh.

Dry white wines are made by leaving the must in the vat until fermentation is complete and all the sugar is converted to alcohol. There are also sweet and semi-sweet (*abocado*) Riojas made by arresting fermentation at the appropriate stage by filtration, centrifugation or the addition of sulphur dioxide, so preserving part of the sugar. A little sweet dessert wine is also made by the addition of *mistela* (a boiled-down must in which fermentation has been checked by the addition of alcohol), but this is not to be recommended.

The Rioja produces small quantities of an acceptable sparkling wine, produced by the traditional Champagne method by the addition of sugar and yeasts to a white wine, with a second fermentation in bottle (see pp. 116 and 131).

VINIFICATION OF ROSÉ WINES

Rosé or *rosado* wines are made from the musts of red grapes, usually the Garnacho, or of mixed red and white grapes. According to the degree of colour and body, the must is left in contact with the skins for periods ranging from minutes to a day or two, and is then fermented *en virgen* (without the skins), like white wines.

THE USES OF OAK

Elaboración, the blending and ageing of wine, has been a major preoccupation in the Rioja—sometimes, the criticism is voiced, to the detriment

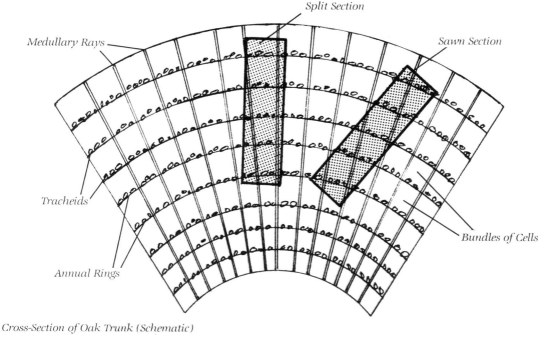

Split Section

Medullary Rays

Sawn Section

Tracheids

Bundles of Cells

Annual Rings

Cross-Section of Oak Trunk (Schematic)

Cells at Surface of Stave (Schematic)

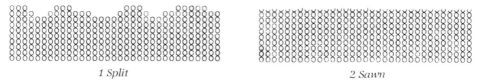

1 Split   *2 Sawn*

of other considerations—since it was so widely practised by the French *négociants.*

Ageing takes place in two stages, first in oak casks and then in bottle. The importance of the first stage is that the wine undergoes slow and controlled oxidation from air entering the cask through the pores of the wood and also picks up tannin and flavouring elements, notably vanillin, the net result of a complex series of chemical reactions being that it gains both in the complexity of bouquet and flavour.

Oak is of such paramount importance in making fine wines, especially red—both because it supplies the materials for the casks and also the corks, in the form of the bark from the cork oak (*Quercus suber*) widely grown in Spain—that more detailed consideration of its role seems justified. This is particularly relevant to the Rioja, since, as Don Manuel Ruiz Hernández has written in his *Estudios sobre el vino de Rioja:*

From 1971 onwards, the bodegas have vastly increased their ageing capacity, using new wood which imparts characteristics to the wine other than the traditional. The wine should possess the typical aroma of fruit and of a particular grape variety, together with discreet and agreeable overtones of oak; what is not acceptable is the presence of an oaky nose and flavour overpowering those which emanate from the grape and ageing process.

The accompanying figure shows a cross-section of the wood used for the staves of the cask. Laboratory experiments have demonstrated that, because of the direction in which the wood is cut, wine is not readily absorbed along the medullary rays, the annual rings or the tracheids, but takes place almost entirely in the bundles of cells near the inner surface of the cask.

There is a marked difference between staves which have been sawn or split; sawing results in the rupture of the cells and increased absorption of the wine, so that new casks made of split wood impart a less aggressive flavour. Because of the predominance of new casks in the large modern bodegas, experiments have been carried out with the interior coating of the casks to reduce absorption. Permanent sealing defeats its own object, rendering the wood physically and chemically inert, but promising results have been obtained by treatment with dilute sodium carbonate solution, followed by thorough washing and stoving.

Another interesting factor which has come to light in experiments carried out at the Estación de Viticultura y Enologia in Haro is the 'auto-destruction' of oak under certain conditions, leading to the evolution of acetic acid; and this may well have a bearing on the high volatile acidity of some wines subjected to prolonged ageing in cask.

Volatile acidity or 'V.A.' is something of a dirty word among Masters of Wine and other connoisseurs. It refers to the presence in unacceptable quantity of volatile acids, mainly acetic, as opposed to 'fixed' and odourless acids, like tartaric. Perhaps for the reason given above, it most often occurs in wines aged for long periods in cask and may give them a sharpish, vinegary nose and flavour. Limits for volatile acidity are set by the Consejo Regulador (see p. 50), varying according to the age of the wine. A trace of volatile acidity is more or less inevitable in wine with long age in cask, and if it is not too pronounced and the wine has plenty of fruit and depth, my own feeling is that too much fuss is sometimes made about it. But, of course, any marked pungency ruins a wine, whatever its other attributes.

Of the different types of oak, the most suitable are American and the French Limousin, between which there is little to choose, both conferring

Oak tinas
at Bodegas
La Rioja Alta

more aroma than the Spanish or Yugo-Slavian. Spanish oak contributes little to the wine and is therefore not used, although the bark from the native cork oak provides excellent corks. Perhaps because American oak has for so long been imported for maturing sherry, it is the favoured type in the Rioja.

Apart from the origin of the wood and the age of the cask, its size is also of relevance. The rate of maturation is directly proportional to the surface area of the container, which decreases rapidly in proportion to its capacity as the size is increased. Wine kept in large barrels or vats therefore matures very slowly. Most of the large *tinas* (vats) and *cuvas* (barrels) used in the preliminary stages are in any case more than fifty years old and deposits of tartrate have long since blocked the pores and coated the surface, so that they function as little more than containers for storage. Similarly, the older oak *barricas* used for the later stages of maturation in bodegas such as López de Heredia and Murrieta, are much gentler on the wine than new casks, and a year or two in new wood may well impart a more pronounced and harsher flavour of oak on the wine, than, for example, half-a-dozen in older wood.

AGEING

When the wine is transferred to 225-litre *barricas* some six months after vinification, it is first stoppered with a glass *obturador*, allowing for the escape of any residual gas. It is thereafter hermetically sealed, and racking or decantation from the lees into fresh casks is carried out every three or four months. Once emptied, the casks are cleaned for further use by a jet of water and by rocking up and down on a wooden floor, and a steel chain is used to scour the sides. The cask is then disinfected, either by burning a sulphur candle inside it or with sulphur dioxide gas from a cylinder.

Some eighteen months after the harvest, six in large vats and a year in *barricas*, the wine has been stabilized and will not grow turbid in the bottle or throw a marked sediment. The youngest of the *crianza* wines, the 3° año, are bottled at this stage, but the older and, of course, the *reservas* and *gran reservas* remain much longer in cask, racking being carried out at progressively longer intervals.

The underground cellars of the old bodegas are tunnelled into the chalky clay and are ideal for the maturing of wine. One of the most impressive is El Calado at López de Heredia, 17 m below ground and 200 m long, where the temperature of 12°C and relative humidity of 80° remain unchanged the year round. The high humidity of a cellar like this leads to an entirely different reaction between the wine, the wood of the cask and the atmosphere than is the case in Jerez, where the cellars are still cool, but above ground and much drier.

In Jerez, slow transpiration through the wall of the cask results in preferential evaporation of water and gradual increase in the strength of the wine; in the Rioja, it is alcohol which is preferentially evaporated into the damp surroundings, so that the wine very gradually decreases in strength. At first sight, the serried casks, tiered five high, resemble a sherry *solera*, but Rioja is never made by the progressive blending of the contents of individual casks; and blending of wines (and, in the case of vintage wine, not more than fifteen per cent of wine of a different year may be blended) is carried out in bulk.

For all their automated and computerized equipment, enabling a small staff to control the different stages of vinification from a central console, ageing at the modern bodegas proceeds along traditional lines in the 225-litre *barricas*, racking being carried out by hand at corresponding expense. However, the ageing floors at establishments like Olarra and Berberana usually occupy a single vast area, that at Olarra extending to 8000 sq m and accommodating 40,000 casks. The otherwise rigorously traditional Muga arranges matters differently, housing the casks above ground in a store insulated with fibre glass.

Towards the end of its period in cask the wine must be clarified or fined. The traditional method for red wines, and still the gentlest and best, as practised at bodegas such as López de Heredia, Riscal and Muga, is to add beaten-up egg-white in the proportion of two whites per hectolitre. The wine becomes suddenly turbid, but as the egg-white settles out, it carries down with it any fine particles, leaving the wine clear and brilliant with an enhanced and cleaner aroma. White wines aged in oak are fined in similar fashion with casein or milk albumen, which lighten the yellow or golden colour acquired from the oak.

On a larger commercial scale, fining is carried out with isinglass or gelatine, and the wine is finally filtered through kieselguhr or sheets of gelatine or, alternatively centrifuged to give it the required brilliance; and the bodegas often refrigerate their white wines to precipitate solid matter.

Pasteurization or the less drastic 'hot-bottling' to improve the keeping qualities is restricted to the cheaper and younger wines intended for early consumption, since it kills all the living matter and interferes with the further development of a fine wine in bottle.

*rt of the
derground
lars of the
arqués de
scal*

*Racking red Rioja
from the lees*

BOTTLING

Except in the case of rare *reservas*, bottling is carried out on a mechanized line or *tren* — surely the noisiest and most boring part of any wine-making establishment, but one in which the owners take a particular pride in showing to visitors, presumably because of its size and mechanical ingenuity, and the expense of installing it.

The wine is pumped up from the casks into large stainless-steel tanks and automatically filled into bottles, previously washed and dried, which are then corked, capsuled and labelled mechanically; and the bottles may then be cartoned forthwith and removed by a forklift truck to spend a further period of ageing.

In the case of the better vintage wines, capsuling and labelling are deferred and the bottles are returned to the cool *calados* for a further period of years and binned away on their sides. The perfectionist López de Heredia bottles its wines in the cellars so as to subject the contents of the casks to the minimum of disturbance and maintain continuity of temperature.

Bottling necessarily involves exposure to air and causes a temporary diminution in bouquet and flavour brought about by oxidation, and a period of six months in bottle is required before they are fully restored.

Once the oxygen dissolved in the wine or trapped in the air between the liquid and the cork has been consumed, a new and complex series of chemical reactions, including chemical reduction, sets in, still further improving the fragrance and fruity flavour of the wine. With the emphasis on long maturation in oak, the importance of bottle-ageing has been under-estimated in the Rioja, and until recently bodegas such as the Marqués de Murrieta released their wines more or less straight from the cask, leaving it to the customer to age them in bottle. For a limited period, Riscal even returned them to the *barrica* after a period in bottle – but this, it transpires, was a temporary expedient necessitated by a shortage of cellarage. The wines, oddly enough, do not appear to have suffered.

The young and inexpensive *vinos sin crianza* are wines of the last harvest without age either in cask or bottle; the youngest of the red *crianza* wines, with the legal minimum of one year in cask, are given up to six months in bottle to recover from the disturbance of the bottling operation. The present tendency with the red *reservas* and *gran reservas* is to reduce the time in cask (though they usually remain in oak for considerably longer than for comparable French wines: see pp. 51 and 52) and to extend the period of bottle-ageing.

The periods of ageing in oak and bottle vary a great deal from bodega to bodega according to the house-style of their wines. For example, those from the Marqués de Cáceres are matured very much along Bordeaux lines, and at Riscal, too, there is emphasis on maturation in bottle. The traditional oaky Riojas from the old-established bodegas in the Barrio de la Estación in Haro, such as López de Heredia and La Rioja Alta, spend much longer in cask—an old *reserva* from López de Heredia may well spend six years in cask and as many or more in bottle. It must, however, be borne in mind that wines such as these spend only a relatively brief period in new oak and are soon racked into older casks, where maturation proceeds at a much reduced rate.

6 INTO THE GLASS

VINTAGES

As has already been explained (p. 66), vintages vary rather less than those in Bordeaux; this is attributable to the geography of the region and to more predictable climatic conditions. It also results from the blending of wine from the sunnier Rioja Baja with those from the other two sub-regions in poor years and, in the past, from the admixture of wine of different vintages (see p. 52).

A comparison of vintages in the Rioja and Bordeaux shows that, though there have been exceptions, both regions have tended to make their best wines in the same years. Examples of this correspondence have been the good or outstanding vintages of 1900, 1915, 1920, 1922, 1924, 1934, 1942, 1947, 1948, 1949, 1953, 1964, 1968, 1970, 1973, 1975, 1976, 1978, 1980 and 1982.

Because of differences in microclimate and the handling of the harvest by different bodegas, any ratings for the Rioja as a whole must be somewhat rought and ready – for example, Riscal made an excellent wine in 1971, and C.V.N.E. in the generally disastrous 1977. Ratings for the earlier years, compiled from the records of the Estación de Viticultura y Enología and other sources, follow:

see p. 66 ... see p. 52

1900 good	1904 very good	1908 average
1901 average	1905 average	1909 average
1902 average	1906 good	1910 good
1903 average	1907 average	1911 good

*The famous
'Catedral' (or
bottle store) at
the Marqués de
Riscal*

1912 average	1933 average	1954 average
1913 average	1934 excellent	1955 very good
1914 average	1935 good	1956 good
1915 very good	1936 average	1957 average
1916 average	1937 average	1958 good
1917 good	1938 excellent	1959 very good
1918 average	1939 average	1960 good
1919 good	1940 average	1961 average
1920 excellent	1941 good	1962 very good
1921 good	1942 excellent	1963 very good
1922 excellent	1943 very good	1964 excellent
1923 average	1944 good	1965 good
1924 excellent	1945 average	1966 average
1925 very good	1946 average	1967 average
1926 average	1947 very good	1968 excellent
1927 average	1948 excellent	1969 average
1928 good	1949 very good	1970 excellent
1929 average	1950 very good	1971 average
1930 average	1951 good	1972 poor
1931 very good	1952 excellent	1973 good
1932 average	1953 average	

The quality of the vintages in the last ten years has, with the exception of 1977, been generally good and sometimes outstanding, though between 1975 and 1978 the amounts of wine produced were much below average.

1973   An abnormal year in the Rioja, somewhat sunless and very windy. The wines were, nevertheless, surprisingly good, if on the light side, but have not always lived up to their early promise, in some cases losing flavour and body in the bottle.

1974   This was a generally cloudy year, with rain at harvest time. The wines tend to lack body and to be somewhat high in acid. Only a few were above average.

1975   A year punctuated by clouds and rain, but with a splendidly sunny autumn. Some areas had an excellent harvest, and their wines were very good. In others they were only average to good.

1976   Conditions for the ripening of the grapes were not of the best, since it rained heavily in August, but the wines have developed well and are often fruity, soft and full-bodied. The Casa del Vino in Laguardia rates the vintage in the Rioja Alavesa as 'very good'; and certainly the red 'Domecq Domain' is the best wine to have been made by the bodega.

1977   After a promising start to the year, it rained persistently in the autumn. The vines were affected by mildew and other diseases, and

The wines served at the Marqués de Riscal during a week-long tasting of old vintages

the harvest was retarded. Apart from 1972, this was the worst vintage of the decade, and some bodegas, like Muga, made no wine at all. Such wine as was made was thin and acid, though C.V.N.E. produced a very satisfactory red.

1978   A year of alternate sunshine and showers, redeemed by a long and sunny summer. The best wines were made from grapes harvested late in November; some, like the Riscal, were fruity and well-balanced and rate very good.

1979   A promising vintage was spoilt by heavy rain during the autumn and at harvest time. The wines tend to be pale in colour with more than average acidity; and although the yield was very large, the quality was only average.

1980   A cool and cloudy year in general, with better weather in the autumn. The vintage, average in amount, was of good quality.

1981   The first of a series of very hot years, with drought conditions in much of Spain. In the Rioja Baja, this resulted in wines over-strong in alcohol, but in the other more temperate sub-regions the vintage was good, both in terms of quality and quantity.

1982   Another hot and sunny year with good weather at harvest time. Although below-average in quantity, this vintage, as in much of the Bordeaux region, promises to be the best since 1970, with big fruity wines full of flavour.

The hand-bottling of an old reserva (C.V.N.E.)

Prospects for the 1983 vintage are not, at the time of writing, promising. An official report runs: 'Until late July, excessively hot weather in June, together with general drought conditions in Spain, were being blamed for a 30 per cent short-fall in this year's harvest. Since then, violent hailstorms in July and persistent heavy rainfall in August (causing the Basque floods) have led to forecasts of a 50 per cent reduction on last year. The presence of mildew has had a serious effect on white wine prospects, and only three weeks warm sunshine can ensure good quality for the reds. Later reports indicate that, although the harvest was considerably below average in amount, the quality of the red wines is good.

CHARACTERISTICS OF RIOJA

Red Rioja is not, as is sometimes but mistakenly thought, unduly heavy — rather the reverse. As is the case with other wines with long age in cask, such as tawny port, slow transpiration of air through the pores of the oak tends to lighten the wines both in colour and flavour, and I have attended tastings where Masters of Wine criticized them as being 'hollow in the middle'.

Of the two types of red Rioja, *clarete* and *tinto*, the *tinto*, fermented out in contact with the skins, is fuller-bodied and richer in extract — although, in fact, the distinction is not rigid, one bodega's *tinto* sometimes tasting like another's *clarete*. Without studying the label, they may at once be recognized by the shape of the bottle — Burgundy-type for *tinto* and Bordeaux-type for *clarete*.

What is, of course, immediately characteristic of most of them is the pronounced vanilla-like fragrance of oak on the nose. This, again, has been criticized by Masters of Wine as masking the taste of the fruit. In fact, the amount of oak on the nose varies a great deal as between one bodega and another. The wines from, for example, the Marqués de Cáceres or the Marqués de Riscal are not noticeably more oaky than representative clarets, while those from thoroughly traditional bodegas, such as López de Heredia and the Marqués de Murrieta, are markedly more so, being more akin to Chianti *classico*. The really important thing is that there should be plenty of fruit behind the oak, as in the justly renowned 'Viña Ardanza' from Bodegas La Rioja Alta. What is not acceptable is a wine made in new casks, where the oak swamps all else.

The dry white wines made by the large bodegas fall into two categories, as has been explained (pp. 88-91).

The traditional, aged in oak, sometimes for many years, is again oaky in nose and flavour, but not maderized if well-made. I have, however, noticed that, whether or not the taste is acquired, it is good white wines of this kind, such as the old white 'Tondonias', clean and fresh for all their oak, which most appeal to connoisseurs. They certainly stand up a great deal better to highly-flavoured Spanish food than their 'cold-fermented' counterparts; and it is perhaps for this reason that they continue to be the most popular in Spain itself. Without going to the extreme of drinking a white Rioja with six years in cask, one may, of course, opt for something in between, like the 'Monopole' from C.V.N.E. with its nice blend of fruit and oak.

The new 'cold-fermented' whites, with a fresh, fruity fragrance which bounces up from the glass, are immediately appealing, but not all of them, like the white Marqués de Cáceres or 'Faustino V', retain the flavour of fruit throughout the glass or bottle. Some, after the first and very promising fruity nose, turn out to lack flavour, acidity and finish or, as the Spanish expressively say, to taste '*soso*'. Cold fermentation in stainless-steel and early bottling is not a universal panacea; and it would be dull indeed if all white Riojas were to resemble the young white wines of the Loire and Alsace, charming as the style is at its best.

There remains a third type of dry white Rioja, not often encountered, but fresh, intensely fruity and more rounded. This, as made in some of the co-operatives such as that of Labastida, without the aid of modern technology, is in effect a *vino de lágrima* (see p. 88).

Sweet white Riojas, made largely with the Malvasía grape, are labelled either '*dulce*' (sweet) or '*abocado*' (semi-sweet) and are for drinking with sweets. Some of the latter type, like the 'Diamante' from Bodegas Franco Españolas, are pleasant, round wines with an agreeably dryish finish.

The rosés (*rosados*), the best of which are made in the Rioja Alta with early-picked Garnacho, are pleasant and fruity wines of their type and vary a good deal in the depth of colour and body according to the time for which the skins are left in contact with the must.

KEEPING, DECANTING AND SERVING

As is the case with Late-bottled or Tawny port, wines like the traditional red Riojas with long maturation in cask are less likely to benefit from prolonged ageing in bottle than those bottled earlier. Nevertheless, well-made wines, especially those from the Rioja Alta, have great staying power

psuling
tles of an
reserva in
olten wax at
degas Muga
odegas Muga)

and improve with age in bottle. The wines from the Rioja Alavesa mature more quickly, but I have nevertheless drunk 1917 and 1922 *reservas* from the Marqués de Riscal (see pp. 146-8), cellared under optimum conditions at the bodega, which were still near their peak.

Relatively few people now-a-days have the facilities to bin away wines under the correct conditions of temperature and humidity, and one of the attractions of the *reservas* and *gran reservas* is that, after a short rest, they are ready for drinking soon after purchase.

If you wish to lay down wine, you should choose from those without undue age in cask and with sufficient acid and tannin. Among the best for this purpose are wines from the Rioja Alta with a high proportion of Tempranillo, one of the grapes most resistant to oxidation, and a proportion of Mazuelo. As examples, Messrs Laymont & Shaw of Truro recommend the 1976 Muga and 1976 'Vina Arana' (from Bodegas La Rioja Alta) as 'near certainties'; and the 1975 'Viña Albina' (from Bodegas Riojanas), the 1976 'Viña Zaco' (from Bodegas Bilbainas) and the 1978 Marqués de Riscal from the Rioja Alavesa as 'worth trying'. I would add the 1976 'Domecq Domain'. 1982 was probably the best vintage since 1970, and with plenty of fruit, tannin and extract, there is every prospect that the wines will repay long ageing. Wines with a high proportion of Garnacho are not suitable, because its musts are readily oxidisable.

Whatever your choice, it is sensible to open a bottle, say, every six months, to make a note on its development and, once the wine is at its peak, to drink the remainder within about half the time it took to reach that point.

Detailed notes on the wines from individual bodegas will be found in Chapter 7.

Because of their long ageing in oak, red Riojas throw almost all their deposit in cask and rarely need decanting, except in the case of very old *reservas.* It can, however, be beneficial in aerating the wine, so helping to bring out the nose and flavour, if there is insufficient time to leave the bottle open before drinking it.

Red Rioja should be drunk at room temperature and, as a general rule, be opened about an hour beforehand. Riojas differ a good deal in this respect: some of the younger wines improve when opened some hours beforehand and may, in fact, drink better on the second day than the first, provided the cork is replaced. One should, however, be careful about the older *reservas:* some repay opening a couple of hours beforehand, whereas others may fade fairly rapidly, losing nose and flavour.

The best glasses, both for the red and white wines, are the large, tulip-shaped Bordeaux type, which should be filled not more than half to allow for development of the bouquet. One of the most irritating habits in restaurants, even the expensive and sophisticated, is to fill the glasses brimful. Cut-glass, decorative as it is on the table, is not to be recommended especially, as is often the case, if the glass is wider at the top than the bottom. Again, if the glass is thick and the wine a little cold, it cannot be warmed in the hand. Coloured glasses do not allow one to appreciate the hue or clarity of the wine — among its great attractions. A firm with a really excellent range of wine glasses is the old-established Berry Brothers & Rudd, of St James's Street, London S.W.1.

The white wines and rosés, except for the old dessert wines, should be drunk young and chilled, but not iced. The simplest method is to leave them in the door of a refrigerator for a couple of hours before opening the bottle. Wines which are oversweet appear less so when cold.

My own feeling is that there are no hard and fast rules for drinking a particular type of wine with different foods — although obviously one would not, for example, drink a full-bodied red with a delicate whitefish. This is further discussed in Chapter 8.

Attaching the fine wire netting (or alambrado*) to bottles of a reserva*

WHERE IS IT DRUNK?

The largest market for Rioja is in Spain itself, and in 1982 some 80 per cent of sales were at home. Here it occupies a commanding position in the upper bracket of the market for table wines. Every restaurant of any repute, whatever else it lists, offers a good selection of Riojas; and a wide choice is always available in grocers and in the increasingly popular supermarkets.

The traditional export market was Latin America, but countries such as Chile and the Argentine are now themselves large-scale producers of wine. During colonial days this was a problem solved quite simply by a Royal Decree ordering the settlers to root up their wines, but today only Venezeula and Mexico import Rioja in large quantities.

Exports have, however, been more than maintained by shipments to northern Europe, by now far the largest foreign outlet, accounting for some 70 per cent of sales abroad. It is, after all, only natural that countries like the United Kingdom, Denmark, Holland, Belgium and Norway, which do not themselves make wine in significant amount, should be good customers. The bulk of this wine, mostly red, is shipped in bottle; but Switzerland also buys a staggering amount (some 6 million litres) of bulk wine. How much of this is sold as Rioja, and what proportion is blended with locally-made wines to give them body and flavour, it is impossible to say.

Other important markets (detailed statistics are given in Exports of Rioja) are the United States, Canada and Japan. At one time, *sangría* (see p. 134), sold under the name of 'Monsieur Henri' by Pepsi-Cola, was the brand leader in the volatile New York market, but has been supplanted progressively by 'Mateus Rosé' from Portugal, 'Blue Nun' from Germany and Lambrusco from Italy. It is a refreshing summer drink, but is best made fresh in a large jug by adding ice, sliced orange and lemon, sparkling mineral water, a sprig of mint and a dash of brandy to red wine.

The pattern of exports differs widely from bodega to bodega. One of the few to sell more wine abroad than at home is the Marqués de Cáceres, which has developed a large market for its well-made wines in the United States. The United States is also the largest foreign market for the excellent wines of the Marqués de Riscal, and both companies export sizeable amounts to the United Kingdom—perhaps it is of significance that their wines are less oaky and more claret-like than most. The largest foreign outlet for the thoroughly traditional wines of Bodegas La Rioja Alta is in the United Kingdom, where they have been most intelligently promoted by a pioneer in selling the better Spanish wines, Laymont & Shaw of Truro. Other firms, such as A.G.E. and the companies formerly with the R.U.M.A.S.A. group, have developed large markets in northern Europe generally.

Foreign sales have also, of course, been much influenced by the take-overs of the 1970s by international wine and spirit concerns such as Seagram and I.D.V. which, in the face of the steeply rising prices of vintage wines from France, have been quick to see the possibilities of selling decently-made and reasonably-priced Rioja in world markets.

In sharp contrast has been the growing exit of smaller, medium-sized firms, such as Muga and Beronia, whose success has depended on word-of-mouth recommendation and press-reports on the quality of their wines.

COSTING

In 1983, a 75 cl bottle of a typical three-year-old red Rioja was available ex-bodega at an average price of 250 pesetas, broken down as follows:

	ptas
Direct cost of wine (@ 100 ptas/litre)	75.00
Overheads at the bodega	25.00
Ancillary materials (bottles, corks, labels)	32.13
Government taxes	54.12
Gross profit to the bodega	18.77
Distributors' charges (18 per cent)	36.88
	241.90

In a Spanish grocer or supermarket, the bottle might be priced at 400 ptas, but in a restaurant might well be listed at nearer 1000 ptas and, as nearer home, the restaurant prices of wine have caused vigorous protest in Spain.

Despite the cost of transport, high excise duty and V.A.T., the same bottle might be bought at wine shops and off-licenses in Britain for about £2.75 (the equivalent of 620 pesetas), or less, in a supermarket.

Inflation proceeds apace in Spain, and at meetings of the Consejo Regulador there is continuing and heated debate between the representatives of the shippers on one side and the growers on the other as to what constitutes a fair price for the new wine. What is of overriding importance is that prices should be held at reasonable levels; otherwise, the foreign markets, so painstakingly acquired, may easily be lost.

7 THE BODEGAS AND THEIR WINES

The principal bodegas are listed alphabetically according to the three sub-regions in which they are located: the Rioja Alta, Rioja Alavesa and Rioja Baja. Most, but not all of them export their wines, since the *Reglamento* (see p. 50) stipulates that only bodegas with a storage capacity of 7500 hectolitres or more, and not less than 2250 hectolitres of wine in the process of ageing, at least half of it in a minimum of 500 of the standard 225-litre *barricas*, may ship abroad wines with *Denominación de Origen*.

LA RIOJA ALTA

A.G.E., Bodegas Unidas, S.A. (Fuenmayor and Navarrete)

The cornerstone of A.G.E. was the firm founded by Félix Azpilicueta y Martínez, a native of Navarra. With his swarthy complexion, moustache and goatee beard, he was an unmistakable figure and a dynamic business-man, one of the first to sell wines to France at the onset of the *phylloxera* epidemic. With the proceeds he constructed a bodega in 1881 named 'El Romeral' after the hamlet outside Fuenmayor, where it was strategically located by the new railway-line, and later opened large depots in Santander, Bilbao and San Sebastián for the export of his wines.

A.G.E. was formed in 1967 by a merger of Azpilicueta with Bodegas Cruz García, founded in 1926, and Entrena, dating from 1945, whose owner, Melquiades Entrena, shortly afterwards proceeded to the acquisition and expansion of Bodegas Berberana. A.G.E. is now jointly controlled by the Banco Español de Crédito and the American giant, Schenley.

The firm operates a vinification plant at Navarrete and large modern premises on the site of the old Azpilicueta bodega at Fuenmayor, and with an average annual production of 18 million bottles is one of the largest in the Rioja. It possesses only 50 hectares of vineyards, so that the great bulk of the wine is either bought in for maturation and blending or made from grapes supplied by local growers in the Rioja Alta and Rioja Alavesa.

The old-style red 'Marqués de Romeral' *reserva* was one of the best traditional Riojas, full-bodied, velvety, rich and oaky. It was a favourite at lunch parties at the Spanish Embassy in London, and I recall a superb case of unspecified vintage (the wines were then labelled according to the number of years spent in cask before bottling), long-forgotten in the cellars of Peter Dominic, which had benefited from years in bottle. A.G.E. still makes 'Romeral' *reservas*, but less round and complete, and more astringent. A young red 'Romeral' is sold in litre bottles.

The other leading red wine from the bodega is the 'Siglo Saco', so-called because it is presented, like 'Dry Sack' sherry, in a distinctive burlap sack.

A.G.E. also makes a young, new-style 'Siglo White', fermented at 15°C to 18°C from 100 per cent Viura, a semi-sweet white 'Parral, and rosé 'Viña Teré', 'Romeral' and 'Siglo'.

Bodegas Berberana, S.A. (Cenicero and Ollauri)

The firm was founded in 1877 by the family of Martínez Berberana, and the original small building in the village of Ollauri near Haro is still used as a bottle store for maturing the wines. It was bought by Melquiades Entrena shortly after he had sold Bodegas Entrena to A.G.E. (q.v.) in 1967, and in 1972 he embarked on the construction of a modern bodega in Cenicero, which, with its average annual production of 20 million bottles, was to become one of the largest in the Rioja.

Apart from its 130 hectares of vineyards in the Rioja Alta, Berberana next embarked on ambitious new plantations of some 900 hectares at Monte Yerga near Aldeanueva del Ebro in the Rioja Baja, where a high proportion of Tempranillo and Viura are grown, in addition to the Garnacho typical of the area. The company was sold to R.U.M.A.S.A. in 1982 and, like the other properties of the expropriated combine, is now Government controlled.

The elegant new plant opposite the railway-station in Cenicero incorporates batteries of modern, temperature-controlled steel fermentation tanks lined with epoxy resin and a huge ageing floor accommodating 40,000 oak *barricas*.

All of the red wines are made from the same basic blend of 80 per cent Tempranillo, 10 per cent Garnacho, 5 per cent Graciano and 5 per cent Mazuelo. They differ according to the quality of the fruit – the best being used for the *reservas* and 'Carta d Oro' – and the time spent in *barrica* and bottle. All are big and fruity.

The biggest-selling of the wines in Spain is the popular 2° año red 'Preferido', which is not aged in wood and spends only a short period in bottle. The better wines are well-known in the United Kingdom, thanks to energetic promotion by the former shippers, Gonzalez Byass & Co. The quality of the 3° año 'Carta de Plata' has sometimes been criticized in Spain itself, but the wine shipped abroad has always been given adequate time in oak. The 'Carta de Oro' is fuller and more mature, and the best vintages of the excellent fruity *reserva* have been 1966, 1970, 1974, 1975, 1976 and 1978.

Berberana also produces a pleasant white 'Carta de Plata', made from 90 per cent Viura and 10 per cent Malvasía, unaged in oak. At its best the fresh fruity nose and flavour last throughout the glass, but the quality is somewhat variable, and I have drunk bottles where they did not and the finish was flabby.

Bodegas Beronia, S.A. (Ollauri)

This small firm began operations in 1970, working from a bodega in the village of Ollauri. It subsequently moved to a well-designed modern building, islanded in its 10 hectares of vineyards, a mile or so outside the village. Since its recent take-over by Gonzalez Byass, the premises are already being extended so as to increase the present annual production of 600,000 bottles.

Its founder, Don Javier Bilbao Iturbe remains in charge. He is a man dedicated to making good wine in the best Riojan tradition and at times of stress goes to talk to his casks in the cool of the cellars, as some gardeners do to their flowers. The red wines, made with 85 per cent of Tempranillo and 15 per cent of Garnacho, Mazuelo and white Viura, are fermented in temperature-controlled steel tanks at as near as possible to 21°C, so as to conserve the full flavour of the fruit. They are clarified in traditional style with egg-whites and then matured for two years in *barrica* and a minimum of two in bottle. There is strict attention to hygiene, and the walls of the bodega are coated with an anti-cryptogrammic paint obtained specially from England.

The young cherry-red 'Beron', fragrant and fruity with a blackberry flavour and pleasant acidity, is aged for four to six months in oak and another in bottle before being released.

Of the older red wines, the 1978 Beronia and 1973 Beronia *reserva* are a darker ruby red, clean, light and fresh, with good fruit and acid balance, and traditional oaky nose.

The bodega also produces a white wine, made mainly from Viura, fresh and fruity enough, but lacking acidity at the finish. This is a new departure and modifications are under way.

Bodegas Bilbainas, S.A. (Haro)

Santiago Ugarte, who founded Bodegas Bilbaínas in 1901, was the son of a Bilbao *négociant* who dominated the wine trade in Santander and the Basque country. Undeterred by the *phylloxera* epidemic then ravaging the Rioja, Ugarte decided that he must have his own source of supply and proceeded to the construction of a large bodega in the Barrio de la Estación in Haro and also acquired wineries in other parts of Spain, notably that of José Mompó in Valdepeñas. At the same time, he developed vineyards in the Rioja Alta and Rioja Alavesa, now amounting to 250 hectares and including those of El Pomal, Viña Zaco, Viña Paceta, Vicauna, Cores, El Cuervo, La Presa and La Pelea, some of which have given their names to the wines.

Bilbaínas began production of sparkling wine by the Champagne method in 1914 and continues to make 'Royal Carlton' and 'Lumen' in cellars deep beneath the bodega. Its 'Royal Carlton' Brut Nature is an excellent wine with fine bubble and good acidity. It is also the only bodega in the Rioja to make a brandy. Current sales of table wines, red, white and rosé run at 2.5 million bottles.

The wines have always been among the most popular of Riojas in the United Kingdom, and for a time the firm maintained a depot and sales organization in London (see p. 41).

The red wines, matured in the bodega's 13,000 oak *barricas*, include the fruity and well-balanced 'Viña Zaco', and fuller-bodied 'Viña Pomal' and 'Viña Pomal' *reserva*, and excellent old 'Vendimia Especial' *gran reservas.*

There is a refreshing 'Brillante' rosé and a range of white wines. 'Viña Paceta' is a traditional white, aged for a period in oak, while the 'Cepa de Oro' is richer and semi-sweet.

Bodegas Campo Viejo, S.A. (Logroño)

Campo Viejo, with large bodegas in the centre of Logroño, was founded in 1959 by Savin S.A., a combine with wineries throughout the country, and with an average annual output of some 24 million bottles is probably the biggest single producer in the Rioja.

Its 350 hectares of vineyards account for 5 per cent of production, and both grapes and wine are bought in from independent growers and co-operatives. Fermentation of the better wines is temperature-controlled, and some are made by *macération carbonique.*

The widely-advertised 2° año 'San Asensio', unaged in oak, a pleasant enough young red wine, is probably the biggest-selling Rioja in Spain, with sales rivalled only by 'Preferido' from Berberana.

The bodega makes a range of big, fruity red wines, rating its best vintages as 1964, 1968, 1970, 1973, 1975 and 1978. Looking through my own tasting book, I find that all of their wines have given me pleasure, even the 1971, made in a dubious year. The red 1970 'Gran Reserva', made with selected grapes from the Rioja Alta, Rioja Alavesa and Rioja Baja (85 per cent Tempranillo, 10 per cent Graciano and 5 per cent Mazuelo), a big, robust wine, was exceptional; but my outright favourite has been the 1966, with its fruity nose, soft blackberry flavour and lingering finish.

Apart from a white 'San Asensio', Campo Viejo also makes a new-style 'cold-fermented' wine from 100 per cent Viura.

Bodegas Carlos Serres, S.A. (Haro)

Of French origin, the bodega was founded in 1896 by Charles Serres. In the manner of the *négociant* who founded it, the firm buys in wine, which it blends and matures, selling a range of *crianza* wines and *reservas*, of which the best are the red 'Carlomagna' *reservas*, made from 60 per cent Tempranillo and 40 per cent Garnacho. It also produces a semi-sweet white 'Fino Blanco' and rosé 'Topacio' and 'Rosado'.

Bodegas Corral, S.A. (Navarrete)

The firm was founded by Don Martín Corral, grandfather of today's President, after whom its 'Viña Martín' wines are named, towards the end of the nineteenth century.

It now operates a brand new plant at Navarrete, 10 km south-west of Logroño, selling some 1.2 million bottles annually.

Its best-known wines are labelled as 'Don Jacobo', available as red, white and rosé. Best of the recent *reservas* are the 1971, 1973, 1975 and 1978, but they tend to suffer from astringency and excessively oaky nose and flavour, resulting from their maturation in new *barricas.*

Bodegas Federico Paternina, S.A. (Haro)

Federico de Paternina y Josué was the fifth son of an aristocratic wine-maker, Eduardo de Paternina, Marqués de Terán who, with the encouragement of the Baron de Rothschild, a shareholder in the Bilbao-Tudela railway, had founded the Bodegas del Marqués de Terán. In 1898, Federico Paternina both married and decided to launch out on his own. The family had large holdings around the village of Ollauri, and Federico started in the grand manner, as he was to continue, by taking over three bodegas well-equipped with fermentation vats and casks for ageing the wines, with a combined annual capacity of 1 million litres. Within a short time his wines gained an extraordinary reputation and were the favourites of Ernest Hemingway and of the bullfighter, Antonio Ordoñez.

As time went on, quarrels arose within the family; and in 1919, with a minimum of publicity, the bodega in Ollauri was bought by a banker from Logroño, Joaquín Herrero de la Riva, who shortly afterwards acquired the large premises of the Co-operativa Católica on the outskirts of Haro and engaged a leading wine-maker from Bordeaux, Etienne Labatut of Calvet, to mastermind the operation. At the same time, he set up a highly efficient sales organization based in Madrid.

The wines were riding high, both in Spain and abroad when the firm was bought by the R.U.M.A.S.A. conglomerate; but shortly after the take-over, 1972 turned out to be one of the worst harvests of the century. José Peñin continues the story in his *Manual de los Vinos de Rioja* (1982).

It appears that the bodega was holding large stocks of the preceding vintage, and to maintain sales, orders went out from the headquarters of R.U.M.A.S.A. in Madrid that it was to be blended with the young 1972. What the salesmen had not realized was that the young wine had not yet completed its malo-lactic fermentation, and the result was that the 1972 'Banda Azul' developed a pronounced bubble in bottle. Some of it, as I can myself testify, tasted more like fizzy lemonade than wine.

The upshot was that for some considerable period many Spanish restaurants and retailers refused to buy 'Banda Azul', and the whole unfortunate episode went to confirm the suspicions of *bodegueros* in the region over the 'invasion' of the Rioja by concern more used to making sherry than table wine. It should be added that the situation has long since been rectified and that when operations were transferred from the Cooperativa Católica to the huge new plant nearby, there was a massive investment in oak *barricas*, of which the concern now possesses some 53,000.

Since the expropriation of R.U.M.A.S.A. in 1983 the firm, like Franco Españolas and Berberana, has been under direct government control.

The present enormous plant with its surface area of 60,000 square metres, its 53,000 oak casks and storage capacity of 27 million litres in bulk and 28 million in bottle, is designed only for blending and maturation, and all the wine is bought in. Average annual sales run at some 8 million bottles.

The red 3° año 'Banda Azul' has regained its popularity. Among the biggest-selling and most moderately-priced of young *crianza* Riojas, it is good value for money.

The big and fruity red 'Viña Vial', matured for two years in *barrica* and two in bottle, is a remarkably consistent and reliable wine. None of the *gran reservas* of recent years have ever quite matched the 1929, gloriously full and complete at its peak in the early 1970s; the most select is the 'Conde de los Andes', named after a well-known Madrid gastronome.

The traditional white 'Banda Dorada', aged for a period in oak, is still available in Spain, but has been replaced in the United Kingdom by a light and fruity 'cold-fermentation' wine without age in oak (sold in Spain as 'Rinsol'). The bodega also makes a sweet white 'Monte Haro' and a dry 'Banda Rosa' rosé.

Apart from these commercially available wines, Paternina maintains a splendid collection of old and historic vintages. These are housed in the deep cellars of the original bodegas in Ollauri, restored and used for the entertainment of privileged visitors, and remarkable for the brilliant red iron deposits on the tunnelled walls.

In the autumn of 1980, *Decanter Magazine*, in association with the United Kingdom importer, Mr David Scatchard, organized in London a unique tasting of twenty fine old red wines from Paternina. He was joined on the panel by Mr Harry Waugh and Mr Clive Coates, M.W., and their notes on ten of the wines are reproduced by kind permission.

1966 (shipped July 1979)

H.W.   Medium colour, plenty of nose. Complete, complex, good flavour, best of the four [which included the 1979, 1968 and 1967].

C.C.   Similar colour to the 1967, but a little browner. Slightly dry, but has style and balance. Similar weight to the 1967. Complex flavour, long finish. Good.

D.S.   Pleasing colour. More Bordeaux than Rioja on the nose. A delicate and pleasing wine caught at its peak.

1964 (shipped March 1977)

H.W.   Medium colour with a nice, interesting nose. Lighter bodied, pleasant flavour, but some acidity and tannin. Not great.

C.C.   Quite mature colour. Nice nose, still fresh. Well-made but not as rich as the 1966. Finishes well, spicy and interesting. Still developing. Good.

D.S.   Good colour. Full characteristic Rioja nose. A big wine, not ready yet but with great promise.

1959 (shipped May 1979)

H.W. Pale, lighter nose, not a big wine but well-balanced. Plenty of tannin, rather good.

C.C. Good mature colour, nice nose, rounded, soft and spicy. Medium bodied, mature, but no signs of age. A lot of depth. Has fruit and ripeness, and finished long and complex. Rather good.

D.S. Big colour, still plenty of tannin but fruit to match. Very nice wine indeed which will keep for a few years more.

1954 (decanted, resealed and shipped in 1977. The wine reserved for the directors' boardroom at the bodega)

H.W. Medium colour, good full nose. Good fruit, good balance, still a little tannin, good stuff!

C.C. Medium, mature colour. Light, quite fresh, a bit astringent at the finish. Not a lot of complexity but perfectly good wine.

D.S. Brighter than expected. Delightful softness on palate with a surprisingly dry finish. Still very sound.

1947 (shipped April 1980)

H.W. Older nose, not a big wine but nicely-made and a good finish. Tannin remarkable for its age.

C.C. Good mature colour, complex mature nose. Round, soft mature wine with fruit and charm. Complex, delicate, lots of character, long finish. Well-matured but a lovely bottle.

D.S. Big colour with slight browning. A fresher note than the colour indicates, but not a strong Rioja. No hint of vice on the palate, a soft, round old wine. Light on the finish. Fades fairly quickly.

1940 (brought to London April 1980)

H.W. Good colour, good nose, a bigger job, heaps of fruit. Good stuff!

C.C. Fully-mature colour, rich but with delicate nose showing some sweetness. Very complex wine, well-matured but still alive, quite rich with lots of spice. A little 'past it' but a very good wine.

D.S. Beautiful big colour, perfect nose, big round soft wine in perfect condition. Could not be better.

1935 (shipped May 1979)

H.W. Very dark by comparison. Remarkable! Lots of fruit and masses of tannin.

C.C. Splendid colour, not more than a 1962 claret. Full rich and meaty nose. Round, quite full, well-matured. A sturdy wine with plenty to go, but not as complex as the 1940 or 1947. A bit four square.

D.S. Deep colour, just browning at the edges. Excitingly inviting nose leading into a classic old wine with a big, clean-tasting finish. Extremely good.

1928 (brought to London in April 1980. Half-bottle)

H.W.   Good colour, old nose. Old, past its best, still tannin and lots of it.

C.C.   Similar colour to the 1935. Nose is quite full but shows age and weakness. Has begun to dry out and a bit flat. Still a lot of tannin. A big, full, muscular sort of wine.

D.S.   Nice colour, weak on the nose, disappointing on the palate. Past its best and somewhat flat.

1910 (brought to London April 1980)

H.W.   Remarkable colour, very unusual, not attractive but much better preserved than the 1918.

C.C.   Splendid colour, beautiful old mature nose, and a refined aristocratic flavour. Lovely fruit and flavour, still very much alive. A lot of quality. A beauty.

D.S.   Big old colour, quite astounding in its depth. Very peculiar strong nose. A back taste of real quality and style. Not showing its age at all.

1902 (brought to London April 1980)

H.W.   Old nose but the wine very much alive. Same style of flavour to the 1910 but better.

C.C.   Very brown, faded nose. Over the top but a good wine once.

D.S.   Big old colour and nose with the same distinctiveness as the 1910 but not as evident. Quality comes out very clearly in this wine, a real classic. At lunch it proved exceptional.

These last two wines were probably in cask for at least fifteen years.

Bodegas Franco Españolas, S.A. (Logroño)

As the name implies, the company was of French origin. In 1890, Féderique Anglade of the Maison Anglade in Bordeaux, who was shipping large amounts of Rioja to France for blending, began maturing small amounts of wine for direct sale. In this he was helped by a gifted *vigneron* from Bordeaux, Alexandre Lepine. The experiments prospered; and in 1901, Bodegas Franco Españolas was formed as a public company with finance both from France and Spain, and set about the construction of the present large premises just over the bridge across the Ebro in Logroño. The firm was acquired by R.U.M.A.S.A. in 1973, and since its dissolution has been managed on behalf of the Spanish government.

It owns no vineyards of its own and buys-in grapes from the Rioja Alta, Rioja Alavesa and Rioja Baja and also ready-made wine. It has long been noted for light, claret-like red wines, such as the inexpensive 'Diamante', and also for the fuller-bodied 'Rioja Bordon', but the best of its wines are the 'Royal' *reservas* and *gran reservas*, of which excellent examples were the 1968 'Tete de Cuvée' and the 1970. Quality was not, however, always maintained during the R.U.M.A.S.A. period, perhaps because of a desire to boost production and sales.

Franco Españolas also makes a dry and oaky traditional white 'Viña Sole'; a fresh, 'cold fermented' new-style 'Viña Soledad', unaged in cask; and a good semi-sweet 'Diamante' with a dryish finish, which goes well with desserts.

Its pleasant rosés are the inexpensive 'Sin Rival', the dry 'Royal' and 'Rosado del Lujo', and the semi-sweet 'Diamante'.

Bodegas Gómez Cruzado (Haro)

One of the older bodegas in the historic Barrio de la Estación near the railway-station in Haro, the firm was founded in 1886 by the Duke of Moctezuma de Tultengo. His first love was for white wines, and his best-known, the 'Viña Motulleri', was made from Viura and Malvasía. The firm was subsequently incorporated in that of A. and J. Gómez Cruzado. Later bought by Carbonell, the well-known producers of olive-oil and Montilla, it has recently changed hands again.

Without quite the prestige of the other bodegas in the hallowed Barrio de la Estación, Gómez Cruzado makes a 2° año red 'Predilecto' for everyday drinking, a more mature 'Viña Dorana' and a *gran reserva* 'Regio Honorable', of which the 1964 was outstanding.

Its young white wine is also labelled 'Predilecto', and there are a white 'Gómez Cruzado' and a 'Motulleri' *reserva* matured in oak.

Bodegas José Palacios, S.A. (Logroño)

Not to be confused with Bodegas Palacio of Laguardia (q.v.), the firm was founded in 1947 by Don José Palacios Remondo and operates from bodegas both in Logroño, near those of Olarra, and in Alfaro in the Rioja Baja.

It works on 'a co-operative system' with independent growers owning some 350 hectares of vineyards and also buys in grapes and wine. The red wines, made from 60 per cent Garnacho and 40 per cent Tempranillo, are labelled as 'Utrero', 'Eral', 'Herencia Remondo' and 'Copa Remondo'. There is also a 'Distinción' rosé.

Bodegas La Rioja Alta, S.A. (Haro)

The Sociedad Vinícola de la Rioja Alta was formed in 1890, when Felipe Puig de la Bellacasa leased the premises of a French *négociant*, Alphonse Viguier,

Loading bay at Bodegas La Rioja Alta in Haro

in the Barrio de la Estación in Haro, joining forces with four other local growers. Its first manager, Mariano Lacort y Tapia, subsequently left the group to found his own firm, and his old stone-built bodega with its timber-beamed roof has recently been acquired by Bodegas Muga to provide additional space for ageing its wines.

La Rioja Alta made its name with such classical wines as the 'Cosecha 1890' and 'Cosecha 1904', and the perennially popular 'Viña Ardanza', named after one of the original shareholders, Alfredo Ardanza y Sanchez. The early history of the bodega has been meticulously recorded in the *Diario de Bodega* by a French cellar-master, Charles Gallait from the Cantenac region of Bordeaux, a fascinating account of harvests good and bad, day-to-day operations, and the bottling and despatch of the wines.

La Rioja Alta possesses 250 hectares of vineyards and also buys in grapes. The wines are made in oak *tinas* and lined cement vats, and there are 23,000 *barricas* for maturing them. Average annual production amounts to 1 million bottles. Standards have remained consistently high, and the wines are well-known in Britain, the largest foreign market, thanks to their judicious marketing by Laymont & Shaw of Truro, a pioneer in introducing the better Spanish wines to the United Kingdom.

The fruity and pleasant 3° año red 'Viña Alberdi' has for long been sold by Sainsbury's. The full-bodied and velvety 'Viña Ardanza', aged for three and a half years in cask and two in bottle, is a firm favourite both with critics and the consumer, and the 'Viña Arana', of about the same age, is a lighter and very stylish wine. With even longer in cask and bottle, the 'Reserva 890' and 'Reserva 904' are traditional well-made red Riojas with oaky nose and plenty of mature fruit.

The Bodega also produces a traditional white Rioja, the 'Metropole Extra', aged in oak, and the fresh young 'Leonora', cold-fermented, but still with a hint of oak and named in honour of the wife of its English shipper.

Bodegas Lagunilla, S.A. (Fuenmayor)

The bodega was founded in 1890 by Don Felipe Lagunilla San Martín, of a local wine-growing family, and was one of the pioneers in introducing American grafts after the *phylloxera* epidemic of the early 1900s. During the boom of the 1970s it was acquired by the sherry firm of Croft, itself a subsidiary of the English International Distillers & Vintners (I.D.V.), and now occupies modern premises adjoining those of Bodegas Lan on the road from Logroño to Haro.

It owns no vineyards of its own, and wine is bought in locally and from the Rioja Baja for maturation and blending. Average annual production is 700,000 bottles.

Its wines include a red 'Lagunilla' aged for two years in cask and one in bottle, a white 'Lagunilla' matured for one year in oak and also a rosé, but best-known are the red 'Herminia' *reservas* and *gran reservas*, such as those of 1975 and 1970.

Bodegas Lan, S.A. (Fuenmayor)

Founded in 1974 by a consortium from Bilbao, Lan is of the new generation of large modern bodegas, occupying impressive premises equipped with the latest in modern equipment. The red wines are, however, scrupulously matured by traditional methods in oak *barricas*, of which the bodega possesses 25,000, and are indeed the favourites of the Spanish authority José Peñin, owing much to the expertise of its oenologist, José Manuel Aizpura. The company was bought by R.U.M.A.S.A. in 1982 and, after its failure the following year, was taken over by the government.

In Spain, the younger wines, including a fresh white and a rosé, are sold as 'Lan' or 'Lambros', and the *reservas* and *gran reservas* as 'Viña Lanciano'. Abroad, they are often marketed under the label of 'Lancorta'.

José Peñín, writing in the 1982 edition of his *Manual de los Vinos de Rioja*, heads his list of best Riojas with the red 5° año and 3° año 'Lan', distinguished by their fragrant nose and fruity flavour, and the well-balanced white 'Lanceros' 1980. My own note on the 1973 'Lancorta' *gran reserva* runs: 'Clear ruby-orange. Pleasant oaky nose. Light and smooth blend of oak and fruit. Slight trace of oiliness and some astringency at the end, but a nice wine with a long finish.'

Bodegas López Agós y Cía. (Fuenmayor)

Another new, but much smaller bodega, this was founded in 1973, with a capacity of 2,250,000 litres and 2000 oak *barricas*. It makes a young red 'López Agós' without age in wood, a mature red 'Señorio Agós, and a dry white 'Agós Oro' matured in oak.

Bodegas R. López de Heredia Viña Tondonia, S.A. (Haro)

Rafael López de Heredia was born in Chile in 1857, but was educated in Spain, completing his commercial studies in Bayonne at a time when Haro was in the full flush of shipping its wines to France in the wake of the *phylloxera* epidemic. Fired with a restless energy and enthusiasm for the wines, he founded his own concern in 1887, taking over the warehouses of the French *négociant* Armande Heff in the Barrio de la Estación in 1881. His company, rigorously traditional in its methods, has been one of the few that has never changed hands and is still controlled by the family.

The Art Nouveau tower of the offices, with its high-pitched tiled roof and carved wooden facings, dominates the other low-built bodegas in the historic area of the railway-station. Inside, the lay-out and decorations remain as they always were: the winding wooden stairs, the brass-mounted windows of the counting house, the stained glass of the boardroom and the yellowing diplomas of merit from bygone exhibitions, which lines the walls of the Director's room. Long may they remain so!

So it is with the bodega itself, built of quarried stone. Many are the sonorous names of the cellars comprising a great underground complex: Bodega Vieja, Bodega Nueva, Bisiestra, Dolorosa, Bodega de las Reservas, El Caladillo, El Calado, El Frontón and El Cementario. Most impressive of all is El Calado, tunnelled out of the sandstone, 17 m below ground and 200 m long, where the temperature of 12°C and the relative humidity of 80° remain unchanged the year round.

*The Art
Nouveau bodega
of R. López de
Heredia in Haro*

All the receptacles used for making the wine, even the new 64,000-litre vats, are of oak, and the wine comes into contact with stainless-steel only in the vessel from which it is filled into the bottles. It is matured in oak *barricas* for three, four, five or six years, and up to eight in the case of the *reservas*, and clarified in traditional manner with egg-whites. This operation, as well as bottling, takes place in the cellars where the wines have lain so long.

The largest of López de Heredia's 170 hectares of vineyards, providing 50 per cent of the fruit, is the famous Viña Tondonia of 110 hectares. The firm also owns three other estates, Viña Bosconia, Viña Cubillo and Viña Zaconia, planted in the proportion of 50 per cent Tempranillo, 30 per cent Garnacho, 10 per cent Graciano and 10 per cent Mazuelo; like Tondonia, they have given their names to the wines.

Average annual production is 1.2 million bottles. When young, the red wines tend to be tannic and hard, but open out gloriously, repaying long ageing in bottle. They comprise the stylish young 3° año 'Cubillo', and the mature 'Tondonia' and 'Bosconia', of which the 'Bosconia' is the bigger and softer. The classic old *reservas* in traditional oaky style, such as the marvellous 1942 'Bosconia', well merit Hugh Johnson's description of 'sumptuous'.

There are no concessions to modernity, and even the white wines, amounting to 25 per cent of production, are matured for long periods in cask. The dry white 'Gravonia' and 'Tondonia' are bottled in their fourth and sixth years, and the semi-sweet 'Zaconia' *abocado* in its sixth. Great care is taken to prevent oxidation during racking, and the wines emerge oaky, but clean and fresh.

Typical of these wines at their best is the legendary 1953, markedly oaky, but soft and intense in flavour. Another classic of the same type, wonderfully fresh and still available in very limited amount, is the 1964 'Tondonia', made half and half from Viura and Malvasía and aged for six years in *barrica* followed by eleven to twelve in bottle.

Bodegas Marqués de Cáceres (Cenicero)

Enrique Forner, who founded the Marqués de Caceres in 1970, was the son of a Republican deputy to the Cortes. Educated in Spain, he was forced to take refuge in France during the early years of the Franco period and profited from his stay by acquiring Château Camensac in the Médoc and Château Trintaudon in Bordeaux Supérieur and gaining a thorough knowledge of French wine-making methods.

Known as the 'Castilian Fox', he is a man both criticized and admired by *bodegueros* of the traditional school in the Rioja. He was quick to seize on a taste for less oaky wines, both in Spain and abroad, and to do away with excessively long periods of maturation in cask—long the 'trademark' of the Rioja.

In some ways his methods resemble those of an earlier generation of French *négociants*; and the bodega was set up as a 'Union Vitivinícola', relying heavily on the careful selection and purchase of ready-made wine from partners in the enterprise and bulk purchase from the excellent Co-operative de Santa Daría (q.v.) in Cenicero, subsequently blended, matured in *barrica* and given long age in bottle.

The new bodega was planned and sited in Cenicero (with advice from that master oenologist, Professor Peynaud of Bordeaux University) as being perhaps the best of the wine-growing regions in the Rioja Alta. The corks are longer than those generally used in the Rioja, and the elegant maroon labels recall those of his Châteaux in Bordeaux. The fruity, claret-like style was evolved with an eye to foreign markets; and, in fact, the Marqués de Cáceres is one of the few bodegas to sell more of its wine abroad (especially in the United States and Britain) than in Spain itself.

The inexpensive red wines are labelled as 'Rivarey' and the more mature as 'Marqués de Cáceres; the *reservas* are well-balanced and less oaky than the typical red Riojas, with a blackcurrant or blackberry flavour and long finish. Particularly good vintages have been the first, of 1970, the 1973 and 1976. The 1970 was at its peak in 1979, but by 1981 the flavour was more of raspberries or strawberries, and in late 1982 the wine was showing definite signs of fading.

One of Forner's most striking innovations was the introduction of a new-style white Rioja, made from 100 per cent Viura, fermented at 16° to 18°C and unaged in oak. Though many other bodegas are now following suit, it remains one of the best of its kind; light, fresh and fruity, with a nose and flavour more reminiscent of the Loire or Alsace than of a traditional white Rioja, and lasting throughout the glass. It has not, however, achieved quite the same success at home, where the taste is for white wines such as 'Monopole' from C.V.N.E. with a definite hint of oak and more body, as abroad. I well remember introducing it to a Spanish friend in a Madrid restaurant; his immediate and definite comment was '*agua pura*' ('pure water')!

Bodegas Marqués de Murrieta (Ygay)

The romantic story of Don Luciano de Murrieta y García-Lemoine, created Marqués de Murrieta in recognition of his pioneering work in improving the quality and keeping properties of Rioja wines during the mid-nineteenth century, have already been outlined (p. 33). The firm continues to operate from the bodega which he built in 1872 on an estate at Ygay, a few km east of Logroño, off the road to Zaragoza, and has remained firmly in the hands of the Murrieta family. It has, however, just been announced that it has been bought jointly by the Compañía Vinícola del Norte de España (C.V.N.E.) and Bodegas Salceda.

The low, stone-built cellars, at the centre of a *finca* embracing 160 hectares of vineyards and also producing olives and other crops, contain oak *tinas* (vats) and old presses dating from the early days of the bodega and, with López de Heredia, Murrieta is perhaps the most conservative of the bodegas in its methods. Until his recent retirement, the wines were made for many decades by Don Pedro-Jesús Marrodán Sainz, one of the great Riojan oenologists, who set his face against the bottle-ageing of wine at the bodega, maintaining that this was the responsibility of the purchaser; and they were bottled ony immediately prior to shipment. It must be said that, as a consequence, and for all their marked individuality and quality, some of the older wines have sometimes suffered from noticeable volatile acidity (see p. 93).

Laguardia and its vineyards, overshadowed by the Sierra Cantábrica

Unlike López de Heredia, Murrieta ferments the wine in epoxy-lined

*Ripe bunches of
Tempranillo
grapes*

*Emptying the
grapes into the
reception hoppe
at the bodega*

*Casks of old
wine in the
Old Cellars
of Federico
Paternina
in Ollauri*

cement vats, and it is then transferred, first to oak *tinas* and then to 225-litre *barricas* for its long maturation. An unusual feature is that the transfer of wine from one container to another is effected by gravity, and not by pumping.

Some 40 per cent of the wine is made from fruit grown in the bodega's own vineyards, planted with 60 per cent Tempranillo, 10 per cent Garnacho and 5 per cent Mazuelo, Graciano and Malvasía. The rest of the grapes are supplied by independent growers, whose vineyards are carefully supervised. If the fruit does not meet the bodega's high standards, they are paid a basic sum and are then free to sell it elsewhere.

The youngest of the red wines is a mellow and fruity 4° año, aged for some three years in *barrica*. Under the regime of the new oenologist, César Simón, and in common with other red *crianza* wines, it is now aged for a minimum of one year in bottle before being released.

The 1960 *reserva*, currently on sale, spent nineteen years in cask and three in bottle. My note on it (November 1982) runs: 'Very deep ruby orange. Remarkable fruity nose after removal or cork. After one hour in a decanter, the nose retained good oak and fruit, but with a trace of volatile acidity. Smooth and full-bodied with deep flavour and long finish, but some volatile acidity, especially at the end. A memorable wine, but somewhat over its peak and tending to fade. Should be drunk now.'

At rare intervals Murrieta makes a superb and much sought-after 'Castillo Ygay', of which the most recent vintages were 1917, 1925, 1934 and 1942. The 1934, of which I was lucky enough to be given a few bottles, was a completely outstanding wine, intense in nose and flavour, long in finish and with overtones of a first-rate claret. Since taking over, César Simón has limited maturation in cask to four years.

Earlier vintages of the white Murrieta were matured along similar lines to the 4° año red; a deep straw-yellow, fresh on the palate and with a nice blend of fruit and oak, they are among the best of traditional white Riojas. More recently the Bodega has reduced the period in cask and is making lighter white wines from a blend of 90 per cent Viura, 8 per cent Malvasía and 2 per cent white Garnacho.

Bodegas Martínez Lacuesta Hnos. (Haro)

Don Félix Martínez Lacuesta, born in Haro in 1873, studied law at Madrid University and was to become a well-known politician, being appointed President of the Diputación Provincial de Logroño and Civil Governor of Teruel and Zaragoza. A public benefactor, who founded the 'Amigos de Haro' ('Friends of Haro') and was President of the Asociación Nacional de

Vinicultores, he never lost his love for his native Rioja, and in 1895, at the age of twenty-one, founded the firm of Martínez Lacuesta, which remains in the family.

The firm began exporting its wines, mainly to South America, establishing an office in Havana in 1902. In 1937 it embarked on the production of a vermouth and has been supplying wines to Iberia Airlines – for which it is perhaps best known abroad – for the last thirty years.

It possesses no vineyards of its own, and the wine is bought in, mainly from local cooperatives, for blending and maturation. It still operates from the original bodega, with its arched entrance, in the heart of Haro.

Some of the red wine proceeds from vineyards in the region of Hormejilla to the south-east of Haro, which produce much of the Garnacho grown in the Rioja Alta. For this reason, it rapidly acquires a brick-red colour. In general the wines are fruity and full-bodied in character. Those of which the Bodega are proudest are the red *reservas* of 1958, 1964 and 1970, and the robust 'Campeador' of the 1973 and 1976 vintages. Martínez Lacuesta also produces a lighter 'Clarete Fino' made with 80 per cent Garnacho, a range of white wines, including a 'Reserva Especial' matured in cask for four years, and a young rosé.

Bodegas Montecillo (Navarrete)

As long ago as the late eighteenth century the Navajas family owned a tiny bodega with 37 *barricas* in the village of Fuenmayor, then better known for its brocade corsets and silk dress coats. At the time of the nineteenth-century Rioja boom, Celestino Navajas sent his son, Alejandro, to study at the École Supérieure d'Agriculture in Bordeaux, and with his brother, Gregorio, he founded the firm of Hijos de Celestino Navajas in 1874. It was later renamed Bodegas Montecillo, S.A., and control passed to the sherry firm of Osborne in 1973.

Large new bodegas with batteries of temperature-controlled fermentation tanks were constructed in 1975 on the outskirts of Navarrete, and the firm is now one of the larger producers, with average annual sales of some 2.7 million bottles, and 77 hectares of vineyards.

The red wines are now fermented at between 22° C and 24° C, so retaining a full, fruity flavour; and the 3° año 'Cumbrero' has established a reputation for quality, consistency and value. The more mature 'Viña Monty' *reservas* are pleasant, well-balanced reds with oaky nose, good fruit and long finish.

The new style white 'Cumbrero', made with 100 per cent Viura, is fermented for two months at 13° C to 15° C. Unaged in oak, it is an excellent new-style white, light, fragrant and delicately fruity.

The vineyards of Bodegas Muga near Haro with the Conchas de Haro in the background (Bodegas Muga)

Bodegas Muga, S.A. (Haro)

Muga was the forerunner of a new breed of modern bodegas, dedicated not to quantity, but to the production of limited amounts of wine made scrupulously by traditional methods. The firm was founded in 1926 by Don Isaac Muga Martínez and worked from bodegas in the centre of Haro. Before his death he had planned a move to the new bodega in the centre of the Barrio de la Estación, but did not live to see it; and the transfer to the new premises was effected in 1971 by his sons Manolo and the popular Isaac, who is in charge of wine-making.

The new bodega started with only the minimum of 500 oak *barricas* entitling it to export its wines, and though the cellars are above ground and insulated with fibre-glass, its methods are determinedly traditional. All the receptacles for making wine, including the fermentation vats, are of American or French oak; after fermentation the wines spend a year in oak *tinas* and another two to four in *barrica*, according to type. They are fined with egg-white, and the 'Prado Enea'*reserva* spends a further two years in bottle and is encapsuled in wax. All the operations, including cooperage, are carried out by a tiny and devoted work-force, headed by the Muga brothers themselves, so that this, as Isaac claims, is a truly 'artesan' bodega.

Muga owns 22 hectares of vineyards in the Rioja Alta — but is acquiring more — and buys the rest of the fruit from regular suppliers, much of it from Abalos. It is scrupulous about the quality and sold off the 1977 harvest, which it did not consider to be of good enough standard for its wines.

Annual production is around 500,000 bottles, and the wines, mostly red, reflect the care that goes to their making and are among the best from the Rioja. I cannot remember drinking a Muga wine which did not give pleasure. There are two styles: the light and elegant 'Muga' and the deeper-coloured, velvety and more fully bodied 'Prado Enea' *reservas*, both with pronounced Tempranillo nose.

Of the 'Mugas', the 1971 was very light in weight, the 1974 somewhat thin in the middle, and the 1975 a better wine, but a little hard and astringent when first released. The most satisfactory have been the really excellent and fruity 1968, the delicious and beautifully balanced 1973 and the luscious 1976, with more body than most. The 'Prado Enea' 1970 was a complete, rounded and exceptional wine, and the 1973 a lighter vintage without quite the depth or finish typical of the wines.

Muga also makes a little white wine, aged in oak, fullish-bodied and clean with a gooseberry nose and flavour, but lacking somewhat in acidity. A more recent departure has been the production of a sparkling wine, made with 100 per cent Viura by the Champagne method. Originally labelled as 'Mugamart' it is light, clean and fruity with a good *mousse*. The 'Conde de Haro', now on sale, does not undergo *dosage* with liqueur, but is topped up after *dégorgement* with a little of the same wine, so that it is completely dry.

Bodegas Olarra, S.A. (Logroño)

The company was founded in 1972 by a group of businessmen from Bilbao, of whom the principal shareholder was the steel-maker Luis Olarra (one of whose plants adjoins Bilbao airport). The winery, the last of the great modern bodegas to be constructed in the Rioja, is sited on the outskirts of Logroño and began operations in 1978. Built in the form of a 'Y' to symbolise the three sub-regions by the architect Juan Antonio Ridruejo, it is a building of considerable elegance and imagination and houses 52 lined steel fermentation tanks of 50,000 litres, the latest in presses and refrigeration plant, elaborate electronic controls and 25,000 *barricas* for ageing the wine in traditional fashion.

Olarra set out to make wines of quality and engaged as its technical director Ezequiel García, formerly the oenologist of C.V.N.E. It owns no vineyards of its own and buys in grapes from all three sub-regions for vinification and elaboration.

With an average annual production of 3.6 million bottles, the plant is not yet working at full capacity, but the wines (of which some of the earlier vintages were made elsewhere) have already established a good reputation.

Most noteworthy are the red 1970 'Tinto Olarra Reserva', made from 60 per cent Tempranillo, 20 per cent Garnacho, 15 per cent Mazuelo and 5 per cent Graciano, and the 'Cerro Añon Reserva' of the same vintage, containing 70 per cent Tempranillo. Both were matured for one year in wooden vats, three in 225-litre barricas and then in bottle, and are full-bodied fruity wines with good nose and long finish. Of the younger reds with rather less time in *barrica*, good vintages were 1973, 1975, 1976 and 1978.

Olarra also makes a fresh young 'Blanco Reciente' from 100 per cent Viura without age in cask or bottle, a fuller-bodied semi-sweet white, and refreshing rosés made with grapes grown at the foot of the highest mountain in the Rioja, San Lorenzo.

Bodegas Ramón Bilbao, S.A. (Haro)

Don Ramón Bilbao Muga, whose family had been active in the wine trade since 1896, founded this medium-sized bodega in 1924. It now occupies premises opposite Paternina in Haro and also owns 10 hectares of vineyards accounting for 5 per cent of production. The rest of the wine is bought in.

Its red wines, made with a high proportion of Garnacho, include a 2° año 'Monte Llano', the more mature 'Monte Seco' and 'Monte Rojo', together with 'Turzaballa' and 'Ramón Bilbao' *reservas* and *gran reservas*. The young white is labelled as 'Monte Blanco'.

Bodegas Real Divisa (Abalos)

This small bodega is situated in Abalos, a charming village in a small enclave of the Rioja Alta to the north of the Ebro and east of Labastida, screened from the main road by groves of trees, which hide its old baronial houses and majestic church and the vineyards on the slopes of the Sierra Cantábrica.

It makes red wines of some note, mainly from the Tempranillo, including the 4° año 'Real Divisa' and a 'Marqués de Legarda' *reserva*.

Bodegas Rioja Santiago (Haro)

The founder of Rioja Santiago was Don Angel de Santiago, who in 1904 constructed a bodega in Haro, just over the bridge across the Ebro, for maturing his wines, and also a winery near Labastida for vinifying them. During the period after the Second World War, the firm exported large amounts of bottled *sangría* to the United States of America under the label of 'Monsieur Henri'. The *Marketing Magazine* of August 1st, 1969, reported a sales drive for the wine and, while doubting that 'a fairly timid $200,000 budget will allow it [the distributor] to see the day when bleacher crowds at base ball games sip Spanish wines from paper cups and shout "olé" when the local hero slams a liner into deep left field', forecast healthy sales. Although, in the fickle American mass-market, *sangría* subsequently lost out, first to 'Mateus Rosé', from Portugal, and later to 'Blue Nun' and Lambrusco, Pepsi-Cola were sufficiently confident to buy out its supplier during the Rioja boom of the 1970s and remain firmly in control.

Even at the period of the take-over, Santiago was exporting 90 per cent of its wines to the United States, Canada, Japan and South America, and this no doubt played a part in Pepsi-Cola's decision. The firm was also one of the first to employ new wine-making techniques, refrigerating its wines to precipitate sediment and then subjecting them in a thin sheet to infra-red radiation, so raising the temperature to 50°C to 60°C and effectively pasteurizing them. This, of course, killed all the living organisms, harmful and otherwise, and its effect on the further development of the red wines is debatable. Another innovation was the bottling of the wine in distinctive bottles of square section, so leading to economies in cartoning and despatch.

Santiago currently owns 27 hectares of vineyards and produces an annual average of 2.4 million bottles. Many of its wines are sold as 'Yago' (or St James, the patron saint of Spain). The older vintages of the 'Condal' *reservas* are very fine, and a curiosity is the red 'Enologico', dating from the inception of the bodega in the *annus mirabilis* of 1904.

Apart from the big-selling *sangría* (an aerated red wine with added citrus juice or citric acid), Santiago also produces a dry white, unaged in cask, from 100 per cent Viura, and rosé wines.

Bodegas Riojanas, S.A. (Cenicero)

The founder of Bodegas Riojanas was a Catalan, Rafael Carreras Picó, who started operations in Cenicero in a modest way in 1890. Thanks to the good quality of his wines and his energy in selling them in South America, the history of the firm was one of unchecked expansion, and it weathered the *phylloxera* epidemic of the early 1900s with conspicuous success. On his death, the firm was sold to neighbours and friends in Cenicero, Tomás and Fortunato Artacho and Fernandez Bobadilla. The Artacho family is still at the helm, although the company is now controlled by Bankinter.

The present large bodega was constructed with advice from Bordeaux, and there were French technicians working there until the outbreak of the 1939 War. Its most striking architectural feature is the castellated keep in pastiche mediaeval style, with its long views over the roofs to the town to the south and the Ebro to the north.

It is of interest that the bodega has never entirely taken to Bordeaux methods, and part of the wine is still made in open *lagos* (see p. 35), albeit of 50,000 litres capacity, by means approximating to the *méthode carbonique*. This is later blended with must produced in the conventional vats.

The firm owns outright only 10 hectares of vineyards, but also draws on a further 200 hectares in the Cenicero area belonging to shareholders in the firm and providing some 50 per cent of the wine. The balance is bought in, either in the form of grapes or ready-made wine. In poor years, use is made of up to 20 per cent of selected Garnacho from Tudelilla in the Rioja Baja.

Youngest of the red wines is a sound 2° año 'Canchales', the more mature and the *reservas* being labelled as 'Viña Albina' and 'Monte Real'. They differ considerably in style, the 'Albina' being a good representative Rioja Alta wine, brisker and more acidic than the 'Monte Real', which contains some 80 per cent of Tempranillo from the Rioja Alavesa and is softer and quicker to mature, with a big fruity nose.

Classic vintages were 1890, 1904, 1915, 1922, 1934, 1942, 1956, 1964, 1966, 1968 and 1970.

There are various white wines, including a young 'Canchales' blanco, made from 100 per cent Viura and unaged in cask, and a 'Puerta Vieja' matured for one year in oak.

Bodegas Riojanas also markets a separate range of wines abroad under the label of 'Artacho'.

In November 1980, some 350 cases of old red wines from Bodegas Riojanas were auctioned at Sotheby's in London, the rarest coming from the private cellars of the company's Chairman, Don Luis Martínez Marauri. The following tasting notes by Patrick Grubb M.W., Julian Brind M.W., and the author, are reproduced by kind permission of *Decanter Magazine* (November 1980):

Monte Real Reserva 1967
There was general agreement about the excellent nose and flavour.
P.G.: 'Almost old Pinot nose. Lovely lingering fragrance. Good, mouth filling.'
J.R.: 'Unusually clean Alavesa nose. Full-flavoured fruity wine. Silky, good

finish, delightful.' J.B. agreed about the nose and flavour, but felt that the finish was 'slightly short' and that the wine lacked real balance.

Monte Real Reserva 1964

All agreed on the nose (P.G.: 'Lovely, very perfumed. Crushed wild strawberries'; J.B. 'Smooth mature intense fruit'; J.R. ('Marked perfumed bouquet') and also on the flavour (P.G.: 'Good fruit finish. light'; J.B. 'Smooth rich mature fruit and bite': J.R. 'Light, delicate. Good linering finish').

On retasting the wine later, P.G. commented 'It has lasted well and improved, a lot of life', but J.B. felt that it was losing strength and that, although a good wine, it should not be kept.

Monte Real Gran Reserva 1964

P.G. and J.R. liked this rather better than Julian Brind. P.G.: 'Lovely creamy, vanilla nose, vegetable finish. Beautiful balance and great length. Very soft.' J.R. 'Cleaner, fresher nose than the Reserva. Very beautiful, well-balanced wine. Light, astringent, almost claret-like. Good finish.'

J.B. commented on its 'rich fruit' and 'strong bite finish', but detected a slight oiliness and felt that it was 'not quite pure and clean'.

Monte Real Gran Reserva 1960

On J.B.'s scale, this wine rated 'very good', and he noted that it had a 'good nose—smooth consolidated fruit, vanilla.' The panel felt, however, that it was a little lacking in flavour: P.G.: 'Soft palate, clean, but not strong flavour'; J.B. 'Some sweetness, but beginning to dry out and lose some fruit'; J.R.: 'Softer and less astringent than the 1964 Gran Reserva, but muted flavour and a shorter finish.'

Monte Real Reserva 1956

P.G. and J.R. were not polite about the nose: P.G.: 'Cheddar cheese, hint of beef tea'; J.R. 'Pronounced Alavesa—over-ripe'; and J.B. noted 'a hint of oxidation in its smooth rich smell.' All, however, like the flavour: P.G. 'Very clean, good fruit . . . Good length, delicately attractive; J.B.: 'Smooth rich fruit, some sweetness, losing body—still pleasant: J.R.: 'Raspberry flavour . . . good finish.'

Viña Albina Reserva 1956

In its intensity of nose J.B. likened this to Romanée Conti. P.G. found the flavour 'very round, full, still meaty, perfectly balanced with some tannin remaining' and J.R. commented on the 'full fruity, raspberry flavour' and long finish. P.G. noted that the wine improved with airing, but J.B., while considering it a 'very interesting wine', did not think that it would keep.

Viña Albina Reserva 1952

A puzzling nose, described by P.G. as 'Port-like, dried leaves', by J.R. as 'Old—Fortnum's Christmas pudding' and by J.B. quite roundly, as 'oxidised'. J.R. and P.G. felt that the wine was still characterful, but J.B. considered it definitely 'gone'.

Monte Real Reserva 1950

A general favourite. P.G.: 'Lovely fresh fruit, grapey, Very clean, well rounded . . . great finish . . . Still good later'; J.B.: 'Dry, but rich strong fruit nose . . . almost Romanée-Conti richness . . . full-flavoured rich fruit — slight acid inbalance dry alive bite finish'; J.R.: 'Very forward concentrated strawberry taste . . . Long finish'.

Viña Albina Reserva 1942

The oldest and palest in colour of the wines (P.G. 'pale garnet'), this is a wine which should be drunk soon after opening, as its nose ('P.G. 'lovely sweet plum') and more particularly its flavour were fugitive. At a first tasting P.G. found it 'very meaty, but also tannic, which overbears the fruit. Drying finish' and J.R.: 'Rather bitter, but a lot of flavour . . . somewhat bitter finish. Later, fading very rapidly with loss of flavour'. J.B. thought it 'very interesting', but spent and only 'a hint of its former self'.

What did not fully register with me when I edited these notes three years ago was Patrick Grubb's likening of the nose to Pinot noir and Julian Brind's repeated references to Romanée-Conti. I myself had described the nose as 'Alavesa' — meaning Tempranillo. Riojas are sometimes described as 'claret-like with a Burgundy nose', and it now strikes me that that these comments lend support to the theory that the Tempranillo was in fact a Pinot noir, brought to the Rioja from Burgundy the Cluniacs and long since acclimatized.

Bodegas Velázquez, S.A. (Cenicero)

One of the youngest of the concerns in the Rioja, Velázquez was founded in 1973 and occupies a bodega in Cenicero next to that of Berberana and opposite the railway-station.

Twenty per cent of the average annual output of 1 million bottles is produced from its own 50 hectares of vineyards, planted with 80 per cent Tempranillo and 20 per cent Garnacho; it also buys in grapes and wine from the area.

The bodega makes only two types of wine, both red, the younger with a year in oak and the other with longer maturation in cask. Both are given a further period in bottle.

Bodegas y Viñedos, S.A. (Ollauri)

A small company making red wines of some interest, including a 2° año 'Viña Emperatriz', a more mature 'Emperatriz' and 'Vega Delicia' *reservas*.

The nineteenth-century Malvoisin pasteurizer in the garden of C.V.N.E. in Haro

Castillo de Cuzcurrita (Río Tirón)

The Castle of Cuzcurrita in the extreme south-west of the Rioja Alta was built in 1367, and in a document of 1774 confirming titles on its owner there is mention of its *'tierras de pan y bino'* ('land of wheat and wine'). The wines, made from grapes grown in its own vineyards, have been prized for centuries; but it is only recently that the family has sold them on a commercial basis, and they are produced in insufficient amount for export.

In the cellars of the old castellated keep, one of the best-preserved and most beautiful in the Rioja, there is a tiny, but modern winery, equipped with horizontal presses and vitrified steel fermentation tanks.

Its wines, all red, are of good quality, but typically acidic in the manner of the others from the Río Tirón, and are sold under the labels of 'Señorio de Cuzcurrita', 'Castillo de Cuzcurrita' and the 'Conde de Alacha' *gran reserva*.

Compañía Vinícola del Norte de España (C.V.N.E.) (Haro)

One of the best of the old-established medium-sized firms, the company was founded in 1879 by Eusebio Real de Asua y Ibarreta, a veteran of the last Carlist War who, suffering from bronchitis, left his native Bilbao for the healthier climate of Haro and in partnership with his brother, Raimundo, and an experienced wine-maker, Isidro Corcuera y del Campo, built the bodega in the Barrio de la Estación in Haro.

Its first sales director was a Frenchman, Luis Perré, connected both with Champagne establishments in Rheims and with the cognac firm of Rémy Martin; and in its early days the company operated a brandy distillery in Alfaro in the Rioja Baja and produced sparkling wine by the Champagne method, actually setting up in 1887 a short-lived sister establishment in Rheims itself. It also established an outlying bodega in Elciego in the Rioja Alavesa for the production of its 'Viña Real'.

An intriguing historical survival from the early days of the bodega is the mobile pasteurizer preserved on the rose-fringed lawn. A scheme for pasteurizing the wines and sterilizing the bottles was first discussed in 1895 and the noble machine was subsequently purchased from the Bordeaux firm of Malvoisin. To minimise the heavy duties on such equipment, the first plan was to transport it by sea, disassembled as 'laboratory equipment'; but it was later despatched by rail in one piece — minus the chimney too tall to negotiate the tunnels of the Pyrenees. It duly played its part in salvaging one of the worst harvests in the Rioja's history — that of 1901 — but has long since become a museum piece.

The wines soon began winning gold medals and diplomas at the great international exhibitions of the late nineteenth and early twentieth centuries, such as those held in Barcelona (1888), London (1889), Antwerp (1894), Bordeaux (1895) and Paris (1900); and the firm was continuously in the van in expanding foreign markets and making good the damage caused by the 1914 and Spanish Civil Wars.

Of the 4 million bottles now produced annually, 65 per cent of the wine is made from grapes grown in C.V.N.E.'s 480 hectares of vineyards and it is vinified both in the traditional oak vats and in more modern lined concrete tanks. There are some 18,000 oak *barricas* for maturation, and about 3 million bottles of *reserva* wines are laid down in the cellars.

The 3° año red 'Cune', made from 60 per cent Tempranillo, 20 per cent Garnacho, 5 per cent Mazuelo and 15 per cent Viura, is one of the most consistent and enjoyable of the young *crianza* wines, and even the generally disastrous 1977 vintage was of very creditable quality, though bettered by an outstanding run of vintages in 1978, 1980, 1981 and 1982.

The 'Imperial' *reservas* from its vineyards in the Rioja Alta are excellent, well-balanced wines, not too oaky and of medium body. The nose is predominantly of Tempranillo, and this is even more marked with the 'Viña Real', a softer, fuller-bodied and more feminine wine, made in Elciego and containing upwards of 70 per cent of the grape. The 1968 'Viña Real', though now past its peak, was an outstanding wine, as is still the glorious 1970 'Imperial'. Other good vintages have been 1966, 1973, 1975, 1976 and 1978.

A new departure is a superior single vineyard wine, 'Contino', made from a blend of 70 per cent Tempranillo, 7 per cent Garnacho, 5 per cent Mazuelo, 5 per cent Graciano and 13 per cent Viura, grown in 40 hectares of vineyards at La Serna, bordering the Ebro in the Rioja Alavesa, west of Oyón. It takes its name from a hereditary official who for centuries supplied wine and comestibles to the Royal Family, and the 1976 is a big, mellow, full-bodied wine with blackberry flavour and long finish.

The white 'Monopole' has for long been the most popular of traditional white Riojas in Spain. It is made in temperature-controlled steel tanks from 70 per cent Viura, 15 per cent Malvasía and 15 per cent white Garnacho and other grapes. Aged in cask for six months, it achieves a most satisfactory blend of oak and fruit. C.V.N.E. has also begun making a lighter new-style white wine unaged in cask, the 'Blanco Viura'.

Cooperativa Vinicola de Santa Daria (Cenicero)

The Cooperative of Santa Daría, one of the best in the Rioja, was founded in 1963 and adjoins the bodegas of the Marqués de Cáceres, to which it is a principal supplier of wines. The grapes are grown by its *socios* (or members) with vineyards in the immediate vicinity.

The Cooperative also bottles and sells wines under its own labels, maturing some of them in oak *barricas*. They include the red 2° año 'Santa Daría' and 'Valdemontán', made from 70° Tempranillo and 30 per cent Garnacho and Viura, unaged in oak, and a red 'Santa Daría' *reserva* matured both in cask and bottle.

The 'cold fermented' dry white 'Santa Daría' blanco seco is made from 85 per cent Viura and 15 per cent Malvasía.

Unión Vitivinícola, S.A., (see Bodegas Marqués de Cáceres)

LA RIOJA ALAVESA

Bodegas Alavesas, S.A. (Laguardia)

Founded in 1972 by a group of local producers, the company operates a large modern bodega just outside the historic old town of Laguardia. Equipped with lined concrete vats and 10,000 oak *barricas*, it has a sizeable storage capacity of 18 million litres and sells some 2.5 million bottles of wine annually, made from grapes grown in its 400 hectares of vineyards in the vicinity or from locally bought fruit.

The wines are labelled 'Solar de Samaniego' in memory of one of the most famous natives of Laguardia, the eighteenth-century poet, Félix María Samaniego who, as the story goes, wrote his celebrated fables under the shade of a fig tree. To foreign ears, they sound a little naive and are of the style of '*Grano a grano hincha la gallina el papo*' ('Grain by grain the fowl fills her crop'). He was, however, concerned with agrarian reform in the Rioja Alavesa and was the author of a trenchant letter on the subject to his uncle, the influential Count of Floridablanca.

The red wines, made with 90 per cent Tempranillo and 10 per cent white Viura, are almost rosé-like in their lightness of colour and body, and are perfumed, soft and quick to mature. The bodega lists its best vintages as 1968, 1970, 1973 (an exceptionally attractive wine), 1974, 1975 and 1978.

The whites are pleasantly acidic and refreshing; and the bodega is now making a 'cold fermented' wine from 100 per cent Viura without age in cask.

Bodegas Campillo (Oyón)

The bodega was founded in 1961 as a sister company of Bodegas Faustino Martínez (q.v.). It owns 90 hectares of vineyards, planted with Tempranillo, Viura and Malvasía, but these are not yet in production, and it buys in grapes and wine, mainly from the Rioja Alavesa.

Wines currently available include the red 'Campillo' *gran reserva* 1975 and 1978 *reserva*, and the 'Campillo' white 1982.

Bodegas Domecq, S.A. (Elciego)

The sherry giant of Pedro Domecq first interested itself in the possibilities of the Rioja in the early 1970s, when it joined forces with the Canadian firm of Seagram to take over the old-established Bodegas Palacio in Laguardia. The partnership was short-lived; and in 1973 Domecq set up a Riojan subsidiary, Sociedad General de Vinos (SOGEVIÑAS), building a large new bodega above Elciego and planting 571 hectares of vineyards in the Alavesa sub-region. The company has recently been renamed after its famous parent.

The vineyards are planted mainly with Tempranillo and Viura in Bordeaux style, the vines being staked and wired rather than grown low and pruned '*en vaso*' (see p. 75) in traditional fashion.

The bodega is equipped with modern stainless-steel fermentation tanks and, with its 13,000 oak *barricas*, is producing some 3.6 million bottles annually.

Of the red wines, made with a high proportion of Tempranillo, the youngest is the pleasant 3° año, 'Viña Eguía'. The maturer reds are labelled as 'Privilegio del Rey Sancho' in Spain and as 'Domecq Domain' abroad. Current vintages are the 1975, 1976, 1978, 1979, 1980 and 1981. The 1976, with an intense Tempranillo nose and 'cigar box' overtones reminiscent of Pinot noir, its deep raspberry flavour, good balance and long finish, is outstanding. Do not be over-eager to drink it, as the wine is still a little tannic and should be even better with further age in bottle.

Domecq also produces a white wine from 100 per cent Viura, fermented at between 18°C and 25°C and unaged in wood, and is to market another mature red in the United Kingdom under the label of Bodegas Valseca.

Bodegas El Coto, S.A. (Oyón)

Bodegas El Coto was founded in 1973, but has subsequently been taken over by Bankunión. The large modern bodega has a capacity of 6.5 million litres, possesses 7000 oak *barricas* and sells some 2 million bottles annually. Thirty-five per cent of production is from its own 123 hectares of vineyards, and it also buys in both grapes and wine from all three sub-regions.

The red wines are labelled as 'El Coto' (meaning a 'hunting preserve', hence the picture of the stag) or 'Coto de Imaz' (Imaz being an old house in the neighbourhood). They are light and very soft with a fragrant nose, thoroughly of the Alavesa. Thanks to its long years in bottle, the 1970 was an exceptionally smooth and well-balanced wine. Another good vintage was the 1978, with deep raspberry flavour.

Bodegas Faustino Martínez, S.A. (Oyón)

The Martínez family has been making wine in the small town of Oyón, some 4 km north of Logroño, since 1860 and before. In their present form, the bodega and vineyards owe much to Don Faustino Martínez Pérez de Albéñiz, a distinguished Riojan viticulturalist, who began the bottling of the wines in

1931; and the firm, one of the few to remain in family hands, is at present directed by his son, Julio Faustino Martínez. It possesses 350 hectares of vineyards in one of the best areas of the Rioja Alavesa, planted with 80 per cent Tempranillo, 10 per cent Viura, 5 per cent Mazuelo and 5 per cent Graciano, from which it produces 25 per cent of the wine. The new bodegas are equipped with up-to-date continuous presses, batteries of 45,000-litre temperature-controlled steel tanks and 12,000 oak *barricas*.

The bodega does not believe in ageing its wines overlong in oak, and the reds are clean, well-balanced and fruity. The 'Faustino I' *gran reserva* was exceptional in the 1964 and 1968 vintages; 1970 was a soft and fruity wine, though now showing signs of age; and the 1973, with greater depth and body, is now drinking better. The 1975 and 1978 *reservas* are also very pleasant wines, the 1975 having better balance and fruit.

Apart from these wines made by the Bordeaux method and aged in *barrica*, Faustino sells a young 'Vino de Cosechero' made in traditional fashion by fermenting whole grapes in a *lago* (see p. 35). The 1982 is a dark plum colour, with yeasty nose and good blackberry flavour, reminiscent of Beaujolais Nouveau. A more mature 1981 seemed to have lost some of the fragrance and depth. These wines, though young, are incidentally not inexpensive, costing more than a regular 3° año red wine.

The bodega was one of the first in the field with a new-style 'cold-fermented' white Rioja, fermented with cultured enzymes at 15°C. Best is the 'Faustino V', made from 100 per cent Viura and recalling a young white from the Loire or Alsace in its fragrance and light fruity flavour — though it tends to extreme dryness. This is produced with the first 45 to 55 per cent of the must coming from the press and is more fruity and delicate than the 'Faustino VII', for which the grapes undergo firmer pressing.

Faustino also markets a dry and fresh 'Faustino V' rosé, made from 100 per cent Tempranillo and released within four months of elaboration.

Bodegas Murúa, S.A. (Elciego)

The company was founded by Don José Murúa Villaverde, who bought wines for blending and maturing. In 1974 it was taken over by a group from Asturias and now owns a co-operative in the village of Samaniego, where the wines are made from locally grown grapes, mainly Tempranillo.

Typical of them are the currently available 5° año and 1970 *gran reserva* red. Fruity and deep in colour, with a fair amount of oak on the nose, they are at their best when first poured out, but tend to lose their softness and develop a degree of astringency and a hint of 'corkiness' in the glass.

Bodegas Palacio, S.A. (Laguardia)

The brothers Palacio arrived in Laguardia from Bilbao in 1894 and lost no time in constructing a bodega on the outskirts of the town, outside the walled precinct. The long, low building remains by the side of the country road to Elciego, but has been abandoned since Seagram's bought the firm in the early 1970s and built a modern bodega on an adjoining site.

The red 'Glorioso', oaky in nose, round and velvety, and intense in flavour, was a first-rate wine, but bears little resemblance to the commercial wines produced in the new plant and sold under the same label. The rare 'Bodas de Oro' 1923 Reserva Especial was a classic, but is now, of course, virtually unobtainable.

In name, if not in style, 'Glorioso' continues to be the best-known wine marketed under the Palacio label, and the firm also produces a dry young 'Semillon' and a sweet white 'Regio'.

Bodegas S.M.S. (Villabuena)

S.M.S. are the initials of the old aristocratic family which founded the bodega prior to 1900, Samaniego Milans del Bosch Solano. Its majestic baronial house, a repository of old armour and furniture recalling descriptions in *Don Quixote*, adjoins the bodega in the picturesque village of Villabuena, overshadowed by the blue heights of the Sierra Cantábrica; and the most famous of the present members of the family is General Milans del Bosch, who in 1982 led the army revolt in Valencia.

All the wines are red and are made entirely from grapes grown in the family's own vineyards around Villabuena. They are fermented in *tinos* (large oak barrels) and spend a year in cement vats before being further matured in cask and bottle. The bodega is small, with a capacity of some 300,000 litres and 600 oak *barricas*.

Until 1981 the grapes were not destalked, so that the wines are dark in colour and tannic when young, maturing more slowly than most from the Alavesa. They include a 3° año 'Valserrano'; a fruity 5° año with a hint of cedar in the nose; and a good 1970 *gran reserva*, fragrant, full-bodied and fruity, with a long somewhat tannic finish.

Cooperativa Vinícola de Labastida (Labastida)

Founded in 1956 and enlarged in 1965, the cooperative is an unpretentious building in a village to the north-east of Haro, noted for the quality of its grapes and because it was the venue of Manuel Quintano's early experiments in ageing Rioja wines in oak. The fruit is supplied by 158 *socios* (or members)

The original cellars of the Marqués de Murrieta

One of the old bodegas at the Marques de Riscal

with vineyards in the best areas of the Rioja Alavesa — Labastida, Samaniego and Villalba — and the co-operative is one of the few in the Rioja to possess oak *barricas* and to bottle its wines.

The youngest of the reds, higher in strength than most Alavesas and sometimes containing up to 13.5° or 14° of alcohol, is a drinkable young 'Manuel Quintano'. The quality of the older wines may be judged from the following notes made in autumn 1980:

> 'Montebueno' tinto 1975: Dark ruby. Fresh oaky Tempranillo nose. Soft, fruity and well-balanced all the way. Long dry finish. Excellent.

> 'Castillo Labastida Reserva' 1970: Deep ruby colour with orange rim. Very fresh and healthy Tempranillo nose. Full-bodied, excellent balance, raspberry flavour. Good dry finish.

> 'Gastrijo Gran Reserva' 1966: Clean, somewhat sweetish Tempranillo nose. Full raspberry flavour, mellow and smooth. Long 'legs' in the glass. Long, dry, fruity aftertaste. First-rate.

The cooperative also produces a fresh young white 'Montebuena', pale straw in colour, intensely fruity both in nose and flavour, unaged in oak and made almost entirely from locally grown Viura with a little Blanquirroja. This is made, not by 'cold fermentation', but by leaving the grapes overnight in a cement *depósito*, running off the must which separates under the weight of the load and transferring it to a separate vat for fermentation. It is therefore a *vino de lágrima* in the style of the rosés from Utiel-Requena, and is a rounder, more complete wine than those produced by 'cold fermentation' in the commercial bodegas.

Herederos del Marqués de Riscal, S.A. (Elciego)

The bodega was founded in 1860 by Don Camilo Hurtado de Amézaga, Marqués de Riscal, and its importance in the development of Rioja wines has already been outlined (see p. 36). Much of the building planned in Bordeaux style by the French viticulturalist Jean Pineau and constructed by the engineer Ricardo Bellsola in 1868, still survives. With modern additions, it lies alongside the road into Elciego from Cenicero and is surmounted by the solid, stone-built mansion of the Riscal family on higher ground just above. Its most picturesque feature is the series of arched cellars housing the oak *barricas* for maturing the wines and the so-called 'Catedral', a cavernous bottle-store, screened by wrought-iron grills and containing thousands of bottles representing every vintage from 1860 onwards.

The original oak fermentation vats have largely been replaced with concrete tanks lined with epoxy resin, and the red wines (the white is produced elsewhere, in Rueda) are made in the usual way by destalking and crushing the grapes and fermenting them for some eight days at temperatures not exceeding 28°C.

Riscal possesses 300 hectares of vineyards around Elciego, of which 20 hectares are planted with Cabernet Sauvignon, half of it new and the rest old. In the past the Bodega used up to 90 per cent of Cabernet in its wines, but the yield is considerably less than that of the native Tempranillo; and the normal blend for the red wines is now 85 per cent Tempranillo, 5 per cent Cabernet, 5 per cent Graciano and 5 per cent Viura. As well as the grapes from its own vineyards, Riscal also buys in fruit from regular suppliers with small vineyards in Elciego and neighbouring Baños de Ebro, Villabuena and Navaridas.

In common with the aristocratic Murrieta, Riscal releases none of its red wines less than 4° año, but has always given them proportionately longer in bottle than Murrieta. They are traditionally light, stylish and elegant, and more in the style of claret than most Riojas, without undue oak on the nose.

Good recent vintages have been 1971, a light but well-balanced wine made in an unpromising year; 1973; 1976, fruity, full-bodied and quick to mature; 1978, an excellent fruity, well-balanced wine with plenty of future life; and 1981. The 1982, with its deep blackcurrant flavour and plenty of tannin, promises to develop as well or better than the 1970. Of the older vintages of the present century, the Director of the bodega, Don Francisco ('Paco') Salamero Arrazubi, one of the most experienced and respected *bodegueros* of the Rioja, considers that the best were: 1910, 1920, 1922, 1925, 1938, 1942, 1943, 1947, 1950, 1964, 1965, 1968 and 1970.

Wreathed in a species of penicillin, pure white in spring and changing to grey or black as the year advances, the countless old bottles in the 'Catedral' are not, as in some wine museums, simply preserved as a showpiece. They are carefully recorked every ten to fifteen years and many, if not most, are in eminently drinkable condition.

This was vividly demonstrated on the occasion of a recent visit to the Bodega by Mr Hugh Johnson and myself. As an experiment, Don Francisco suggested throwing a 'birthday party', with a wine dating from the year of birth of everyone around the dinner table. In some cases there were large amounts of sediment and suspended matter, and it proved necessary to decant off the upper part of 6 bottles to obtain one of the required clarity and brilliance; but it should be emphasized that the choice was entirely haphazard and therefore representative of the cellar as a whole and its 120-odd different vintages—and not of specially selected wines.

I reproduce the tasting notes made by Hugh Johnson and myself at the time (July 1983) by kind permission of *Decanter Magazine:*

1950

H.J. A remarkable consistency of flavour and style with the 1968 and 1934 tasted earlier, but this vintage is tiring a little, thinning out and losing the depth of flavour of e.g. the 1954.

J.R. Ripe, fruity nose, extremely soft, lacking a little in body, but still beautiful.

1952

H.J. Notably paler in colour than the 1947 tasted earlier (which was 60 per cent of Cabernet). An open wine without great concentration, a harmonious marriage of old Tempranillo and oak, finally sweetish and lacking the astringency to give it a perfectly clean finish.

J.R. Soft with its quota of fruit, but somewhat thin and over the top. The overriding impression was of delicate and very refined oak.

1941 (60 per cent Tempranillo, 30 per cent Cabernet, 10 per cent Graciano)

H.J. After a rather hard, forbidding first impression the 1941 developed a lovely fragrance. It remained firm, light but very long, ending with fine clear acidity. Excellent.

J.R. Very dark in colour. Fully body, deep fruity nose and flavour with balsamic overtones, full of vigour with long finish. One of the best.

1939 (50 per cent Cabernet, 30 per cent Tempranillo, 20 per cent Graciano)

H.J. A quiet wine not giving a great deal: low-profile from first to last. Not bad, but *very* dry (oddly enough, like the weather that year, Paco Salamero's first vintage in charge).

J.R. Somewhat lighter in colour. Still pleasant with refined fruity nose, but on the thin side with some astringency at the end, reflecting in minor key the qualities of the others.

1931 (60 per cent Cabernet, 30 per cent Tempranillo, 10 per cent Graciano)

H.J. Good dark colour but otherwise not impressive at first, appearing weak and tired. It picked up fairly well in the glass. Pleasant, but completely over-shadowed by the 1917.

J.R. A stylish wine by most standards with body and flavour, but less pronounced nose and very slightly corky.

1917 (90 per cent Cabernet, 10 per cent Tempranillo. This was a year when half the harvest was left unpicked, because of a cholera epidemic and shortage of labour.)

H.J. Much the biggest of the last four wines; very dark in colour and still almost juicy in character. After a while in the glass it seemed to become even darker. Marvellous developing flavour, growing slightly cheesey after a while but immensely long with a lovely, softly yielding finish. Quite outstanding.

J.R. An astonishingly dark ruby red. Intense fruity nose and flavour. Rich and mellow, with long and beautiful finish. Marvellous.

Outside the coopery of the Marqués de Riscal

Apart from these wines, chosen completely at random, there are, of course, others in the 'Catedral' that are outstanding. Particular favourites of my own are the 1964, deep in nose and flavour and almost perfect; the 1950, with its ripe fruit, good body and long finish; and the wonderful 1922, on which my note is 'Very deep blackberry colour with orange rim, intense blackberry flavour. Good body and long finish — it resembled one of the best of the St Emilions. Magnificent.'

The white Riscal is of two types, a 'cold-fermented' wine without age in oak and a rounder, more fully-flavoured 'Limousin' matured for a few months in French oak; it is not, however, made in the Rioja, but at a modern winery in Rueda, near Valladolid. The Bodega also produces small amounts of a fresh rosé in Elciego, made in traditional fashion by limiting contact with the skins during fermentaiton.

La Granja Remelluri (Labastida)

Founded in 1970 by Jaime Rodriguez Salis, this is a bodega, like Beronia in Ollauri, dedicated to the small-scale production of good quality wines by traditional methods. It makes exclusively red wines from grapes grown in its own 40 hectares of vineyards, planted with 80 per cent Tempranillo, 10 per cent Mazuelo and 10 per cent Viura. The 1976 vintage is mentioned by the Spanish authority, José Peñin, as one of his favourite red Riojas.

Sociedad Vinícola Laserna, (see Compañía Vinícola del Norte de España)

Viña Salceda, S.A. (Elciego)

The bodega was founded in 1974 under the name of Larrea Rabanos and occupies modern premises built at the time, just across the bridge over the Ebro on the by-road from Cenicero to Elciego. Of medium size, with average sales of 660,000 bottles, and equipped with stainless-steel fermentation tanks, it rapidly established a reputation for its sound red wines.

The Bodega owns 15 hectares of vineyards, planted with 100 per cent Tempranillo, in the Rioja Alavesa, accounting for 15 per cent of the wine. It also buys in fruit and wine from local growers.

The younger wines are marketed as 'Viña Salceda' and the older *reservas* and *gran reservas* as the 'Conde de Salceda'. The first to appear under its label was the excellent 1970, and other good wines, made mainly from Tempranillo with a little white Viura, have been the 1973, 1975 and 1978.

LA RIOJA BAJA

Bodegas de la Torre y Lapuerta, S.A. (Alfaro)

The bodega is highly individual, in that the wines are made in a winery located within a sugar refinery. Its red wines are stout, honest-to-goodness Garnacho growths, the younger being labelled as 'Viña Algodi' and the more mature as 'Campo Burgo'. Of the red *reservas*, the 1964 and 1969 have been the best. The bodega also makes white and rosé wines under the same names.

Bodegas Gurpegui (San Adrián)

This large family firm with bodegas in San Adrián in the Rioja Baja and also in Haro, dates from 1872, but it was in 1921 that Don Primitivo Gurpegui Muro established the extensive bodega in San Adrián. The present storage capacity runs to 14 million litres, with an additional million bottles of *reservas* maturing in the cellars, and some 12,000 oak *barricas* for maturing the wines. Between its large sales of *sin crianza* red wine in Spain, its extensive *reservas* and growing export of the well-made 'Berceo' wines, the company is now among the most considerable in the Rioja. The present owner, Don Luis Gurpegui Muga, is of the third generation of the family.

The firm has large vineyard holdings, variously stated as 450 hectares and 1000 hectares, and also buys in grapes from independent growers in all three sub-regions.

Its most select red wines, made principally from Tempranillo and Garnacho with small amounts of Mazuelo, Graciano and Viura, are labelled as 'Viña Berceo' after the famous brother from San Millán de Yuso (see p. 28), the first writer to use Castilian rather than Latin. They currently include a 1978 'Tinto', a 1976 *reserva* and 1973 *gran reserva*, sturdy wines with plenty of fruit in the style of the Rioja Baja.

The 'cold-fermented' white 'Berceo' is a new-style wine unaged in oak and made with 80 per cent Viura and 20 per cent Malvasía.

The rosés, made with 100 per cent Garnacho, have long been produced by a method well in advance of its time. On reception at the bodega, the whole grapes are transferred to chambers containing sloping wooden slats. Under the weight of the load, the juice is pressed out without mechanical means and runs into the fermentation vats, where it is fermented *en blanc* at 18°C. As with the rosé produced in Utiel-Requena and the white made at the Cooperativa de Labastida (q.v.), this results in a very fresh wine and one of the best from the bodega.

Bodegas Muerza, S.A. (San Adrián)

In 1882, Felipe Ugalde Echevarría moved to Haro from his native Navarra and set up a wine firm. A forceful and dynamic man, like many of his compatriots, he merged the firm with that of Francisco Hormaeche, S.A., and later joined forces with the Muerza family. The firm, now known as Bodegas Muerza, sells an annual average of some 1.2 million bottles. It owns no vineyards of its own and buys in grapes and wine.

The young red 'Rioja Vega Tinto' contains some 80 per cent Garnacho, and the *reserva*, sold as 'Rioja Vega' and 'Señorial', up to 80 per cent Tempranillo. There is also a young white 'Rioja Vega Blanco', made with 70 per cent Viura, 20 per cent Garnacho blanco and 10 per cent Malvasía.

Faustino Rivero Ulecia, S.A. (Arnedo)

Founded in 1903 by Don Agapito Rivero, the bodega now produces between 1 and 2 million bottles of wine annually. It owns 30 hectares of vineyards, accounting for 20 per cent of production, and also buys in fruit and wine.

Its wines include a red 2° año 'Rasillo' and 'Señorio de Prayla' *reservas*, such as the 1970 and 1973.

Savin, S.A. (Aldeanueva del Ebro)

Founded in 1958 and now controlled by the Banco de Bilbao, Savin, with its 4500 shareholders, 950 employees and establishments in Logroño, San Sebastián, Pasajes, Jumilla, Madrid, Alcázar de San Juan, Sevilla, Oviedo and Sansol, is probably the largest producer of table wines in Spain since the demise of R.U.M.A.S.A. It makes both wines for everyday consumption and superior growths, like those of Bodegas Campo Viejo in Logroño (q.v.).

Aldeanueva del Ebro, where it produces large amounts of wine from the extensive vineyards of the Rioja Baja, is not one of the more attractive towns of the region. A place of low houses and long, straight streets, it is bakingly hot in summer and is not, as the name implies, either a village, new or near the River Ebro.

8 COOKING OF THE RIOJA

Wine and food go together, especially table wines like those from the Rioja, which do not always show to their best under the clinical conditions of a tasting room.

One can hardly speak of a Riojan cuisine; the region draws its best dishes from Old Castile, of which the province of La Rioja is a part, and also from neighbouring Navarra and Aragón. In the main, as in other parts of Spain, they are prepared from fresh ingredients in season; and the basis of any meal is a visit to the local market, with its stalls selling vegetables, fruit, meat, fish, charcuterie and the rest.

Much of the best cooking is to be had in the bodegas themselves, where the meal is often served in a large cellar lined with casks or bottles, the blaze from a fire heaped with dry vine shoots and used for grilling the small lamb-chops, so often served to set off the red wines, helping to dissipate the penetrating cold. There are, nevertheless, numerous good restaurants scattered up and down the region; and a gazetteer follows later.

APERITIFS AND STARTERS

In the days when the Rioja was less well-known than it is now, André Simon once wrote that the region produced better vegetables than wine. Certainly there is no better way of starting a meal than with fresh vegetables in season.

The fat and luscious asparagus, much of it irrigated and grown in the Rioja Baja, is among the best in Spain. It is accompanied by mayonnaise or

Stall in the vegetable market in Logroño

sauce vinaigrette and goes well with the light, new-style white wines. *Alca-chofas* (globe artichokes), stuffed or otherwise, and *acelgas*, akin to spinach but rather sweeter, are served on their own, as is the braised and celery-like cardoon.

The best-known of Riojan vegetable dishes are, however, *patatas riojanas*, potatoes in a clear orange-coloured sauce made from the spicy *chorizo* sausage with which they are cooked, and the *menestra riojana*, a

*rious work
 Terete's
staurant in
aro*

mixed vegetable dish. The story goes that when Paul Bocuse was engaged by C.V.N.E. to cook its centenary banquet, he was served *patatas riojanas* prepared by the Bodega's regular cook—and promptly asked why he had been sent for! The *menestra* is made from fresh broad beans, peas, *acelgas* or whatever is in season, cooked in olive-oil and wine with chopped onions, tomatoes, bacon or ham, and sometimes hard-boiled eggs. Both of these are substantial dishes and call for one of the fuller-bodied traditional white Riojas, a *clarete*, or light red wine.

The piquant *chorizo*, so much used in cooking, is also served thinly sliced on its own as an apéritif, and is a highly-cured pepper sausage, not cooked but hung up to dry.

Though not specifically of the region, *tortilla española*, the thick Spanish omelette, is often served cut-up as an apéritif or starter. It is juicier when made with onion. Another lighter and most attractive way with eggs, which *is* typical of the Rioja, is the *revuelto con ajos*. This is not heavily laden with garlic, as the name might suggest, but consists of eggs scrambled with the tender green shoots, with a taste more resembling baby asparagus. The shoots are available from grocers in tins and are well worth bringing home.

FISH

Not being near the sea, the Rioja is not specially known for fish dishes like the neighbouring Basque country. However, there is a plentiful supply of fresh fish and shellfish in the large markets of places such as Logroño, and typical Spanish dishes, like *paella* and *merluza a la vasca* (hake with asparagus tips) feature on restaurant menus. The Rioja's own contribution to fish cookery is *bacalao a la riojana*, dried and salted cod cooked with olive oil, garlic, strips of fresh or canned red pepper and paprika powder. An oaky and traditional white 'Tondonia' or Murrieta will stand up well to the rich assortment of flavours.

There is also trout from the mountain streams, often served by slitting open the fish and inserting a slice of ham. In this form it is sometimes, but mistakenly, described as *trucha a la Navarra*.

CHICKEN AND GAME

Chicken is prepared in a variety of styles, such as the *pollo a la chilindrón* in its spicy orange-coloured sauce, made with onions, tomatoes and peppers, a creation of bordering Aragón. There is also plentiful game in the shape of quail, pheasant, partridge and rabbits from the surrounding hills, and a speciality is the tiny *malvices* (red-wing), fried whole. The normal choice of wine is a *clarete* or one of the lighter *tintos*.

MEAT

Everywhere in the Rioja, especially in the Rioja Baja, you will see the wandering flocks of sheep; and the favourite forms of meat are the *chuletas de cordero* (small lamb-chops) and the *cordero lechal asado* (roast milk-fed lamb), also known as *lechazo*. The chops are grilled by kindling a fire of dry vine shoots, the cuttings from the vineyards, raking it out and placing a large metal grid

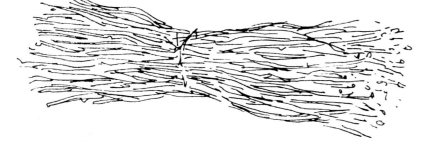

Dry vine shoots used for grilling lamb chops

A flock of sheep, so typical of the Rioja Baja

over the glowing embers. They are tossed once or twice during cooking and end up with a delicious smokey flavour. The milk-fed lamb is smaller and tenderer than any available in England and is best cooked by roasting it in a hot baker's oven. *Cabrito asado* (roast kid) is cooked in the same way, and any of these dishes will bring out the qualities of a good, full-bodied red *reserva*.

The ubiquitous *chorizo* appears as a main dish or entrée in the form of *chorizo a la brasa*, in which it is roasted whole, or as *picadillo* in which it is ground before being cooked. Both dishes are extremely hot and spicy and call for a chilled dry white wine. Another cured sausage, *morcilla*, made with onions and savoury rice, is somewhat akin to the Scots black pudding, but may also be prepared in the form of *morcilla dulce* with cinammon, spices and a little sugar. In this form it is usually eaten as a starter — but nothing short of a sweet or semi-sweet (*abocado*) white wine will go with it.

No less hot and spicy than the *picadillo* are the *callos a la riojana* (Riojan-style tripe), warming and appetizing enough on a cold day, but not something to serve with a vintage wine!

A better companion to a good *clarete* or red wine is the *mollejas de ternera empanadas* (sweetbread fritters). These are sometimes served on a platter with crisp-fried squares of brains, testicles, and with small lamb-cutlets. A most delicious combination it is, but you should order it only in a restaurant where hygiene is of a high standard.

MIXED DISHES

There are a number of these, and though the English would no doubt refer to them as 'made up dishes', they can be delicious. Thoroughly typical are the *pimientos rellenos a la riojana*, a local variant on stuffed peppers, filled with a mixture of ground pork, beaten egg, nutmeg, garlic, parsley and a little pepper and salt, fried in hot olive-oil and served in a piquant sauce. It requires a full-bodied and robust *tinto* to match it.

Another rib-warming and essentially peasant dish, much eaten by the workers in the vineyards, but excellent of its kind, is the *pochas riojanas*. This takes its dark red colour from the *chorizo* with which it is cooked and is a nourishing stew made with a local variety of the haricot bean, allowed to fatten in the pod, but not dried. Wash it down with the local house wine.

Spanish pasta is good, though sometimes different in style from the Italian, and is made in considerable variety. The *canalones* are often particularly appetizing.

SWEETS

The Rioja and Spain generally do not boast any great variety of sweets. The best-known are the well-made *flan* (caramel cream); *torrijas*, a confection served with warm honey and ground almonds and made by soaking slices of bread in sherry, sugar and cinammon, dredging them in beaten egg and frying them crisp in olive-oil; and *leche frita*, fried strips or squares of bechamel, sweetened with sugar and flavoured with cinammon.

A pleasant way of finishing the meal is with *melocotones en almíbar*, large and luscious locally-grown peaches preserved in syrup, or with fresh fruit in season.

There is a good local goat cheese, Roncal from neighbouring Navarra, mature, firm, with plenty of bite and a good nutty flavour, and Manchego, a hard ewe's milk cheese from La Mancha, is always available. Both are often eaten with *membrillo*, a dark brown quince paste.

RESTAURANTS

Alfaro

Palacios, Zaragoza road, km 232; Tel. 18 01 00. In the Hotel Palacios in Alfaro at the extreme east of the Rioja Baja, the restaurant serves regional dishes and has a good wine list.

Arnedo

* *Sopitas*, Carreras, 4; Tel. 38 02 66. One of the most atmospheric restaurants in the Rioja, Sopitas is literally tunnelled into the great red sandstone cliffs overhanging this picturesque little town in the Rioja Baja, and is divided into small alcoves with swing-doors giving off the main chamber. The cooking matches the surroundings, specialities being the *revuelto de ajo* (scrambled egg with garlic shoots), *malvices* (fried red-wing) and *cabrito asado* (roast baby kit).

Calahorra

La Taberna de la Cuarta Esquina, De las Cuatro Esquinas, 16; Tel. 13 43 55. In the largest of the towns of the Rioja Baja, La Taberna serves *revuelto de ajo* (scrambled egg with garlic shoots), *migas* (fried breadcrumbs), *lechazo* (roast baby lamb) and *bacalao* (dried cod).

Montserrat, Manuel Falla, 7; Tel. 13 00 17. Its specialities are *pimientos rellenos a la riojana* (stuffed peppers), langoustines and *miel y mató* (cream with honey and nuts).

Cenicero

Bar-Restaurant Conchita Adjoining the large bodegas of this wine centre in the Rioja Alta, the tiny and intimate Conchita is run by a former catering manager of Bodegas Berberana and serves excellently prepared local dishes. One of Loly's triumphs is the *pochas* (haricot beans) stewed with *chorizo*.

The menu of Sopitas in Arnedo – prices are still very reasonable

MENU DE LA CASA
eran facilitados en hojas aparte y cuyo importe
o excedera del 80% del importe en carta de los
platos que lo compongan.
Incluido, pan, vino y postre.

RESTAURANTE
" SOPITAS "
(3.ª CATEGORIA)
CARRERA, 4   ARNEDO

Primer Grupo - Entremeses y Sopas

ENTREMESES

Jamón ....(50 g.)	160
Lecherillas	260
Picadillo	160
Espárragos	200
Setas	210
Champiñon	160
Gordillas	150
Revuelto de ajos	190
Ensalada corriente	70
Ensalada ilustrada	150
Sesos	235
Pechuga de Pollo a la Romana	160
Caracoles	150
ENTREMES	250
Espárragos Extra	250
Chorizo	150

SOPAS CONSOME   85

De cocido	
De pescado	125
De ajo	
CONSOME CON VENA O JEREZ	100

Segundo Grupo - Verduras, Huevos y Pescados

VERDURAS

Cardo	125
Habas CON JAMON	125
Coliflor	125
Berza	
Borraja	125
Alcachofas	145
Alcachofas albardadas	175
Alubia verde	125
Pochas	
Arroz	150
Paella especial encargo	300
Menestra	285
Menestra extra especial encargo	310
Garbanzos	
Alubias	
Caparrón	

HUEVOS

Huevos fritos	120
Huevos rellenos	
Huevos con tomate	100
Huevos fritos con pimientos	135
Huevos fritos con patatas fritas	135
Huevos en tortilla	120
Huevos en tortilla con bonito	140
Huevos en tortilla con espárragos	150
Huevos en tortilla con jamón	140
Huevos en tortilla con chorizo	140
Huevos en tortilla con patatas	150

PESCADO

MERLUZA A LA UASCA	550
Trucha	260
Merluza	385
Angulas	500
Langostinos	450
Gambas	
Calamares en su tinta	
Almejas a la marinera	250
BACALAO A LA RIOJANA	230

Tercer Grupo - Carnes y Aves

CARNES

CONEJO	250
Chuletas de cordero	250
Chuletas de ternera	425
Chuletas de lomo	250
Filete de ternera (solomillo)	425
Filete de lomo	250
Cabrito asado	550
Pollo en su jugo	150
Pollo en salsa	150
Malvices	250
Codornices	250
Perdiz ENTERA	250
Cabeza asada	125
Callos	
Patitas	

Cuarto Grupo - Postres

Frutas varias	80
Melocotón en almíbar	80
Piña	80
Tarta DE la casa	110
Fardelejos	120
Helado	100
Tarta helada o croCanti	110
Pera en almíbar	80
Nueces	100
Copa de la casa	110
Fresas	150
Queso	100

VINOS

Comunes de 3/4 tinto	110
Comunes de 3/4 clarete	110
Sangría	150
Cerveza 1/5	88
Cerveza 1/3	42
Coca-Cola	34
Agua mineral un litro	60
Pan un bollo	12
1/2 litro agua mineral	30

CAFES

Café solo	32
Café con leche	35
Vaso de leche	30

SERVICIOS E IMPUESTOS INCLUIDOS

EN ESTE ESTABLECIMIENTO EXISTE HOJAS DE RECLAMACIONES
IL Y A DES FEULLES DE RECLAMATIONS A DIS POSITION DES CLIEN
THERE IS AN AFFCIAL FOLIOS FOR CLIENTS CLAIMS

Gráficas Isasa-Arnedo

Ezcaray

Ezcarray is a small winter sports resort in the mountains near the Monasteries of Suso and Yuso and boasts two of the best restaurants in the region. As they are small, it is preferable to book beforehand.

* *Hostal Echaurren*, General Mola, 2; Tel. 35 40 47. This old posting house, converted into a comfortable restaurant, attracts a clientèle from as far as Bilbao. It offers excellent fish soup, *merluza óptima* (hake), *alcachofas* (artichokes) and fresh Riojan vegetables, *lechazo* (roast baby lamb), *redondo de ternera* (baked roll of veal) and good house wines from the Rioja.

* *Hostal Marichu*, Avda. de Jesús Nazareno; Tel. 35 40 05. As the Hostal is full all the year round, you may have to wait your turn in the quiet garden. The menu is short but first-rate and includes *alubias* (beans), *merluza perfecta* (hake), good roast meats and excellent home-made sweets.

Fuenmayor

El Porrón, Avda. de Cenicero, 42; Tel. 45 00 52. This is a restaurant in a flourishing wine centre of the Rioja Alta, much patronized by the *bodegueros*. Among its specialities are *patatas a la riojana* (potatoes in spicy sauce), *chuletas de cordero* (lamb-chops grilled over vine shoots) and *flan* (cream caramel). There is a long list of Rioja wines.

Haro

There are two excellent restaurants in Haro, the wine capital of the Rioja Alta.

* *Beethoven II*, Santo Tomás, 3; Tel. 31 11 81. Oddly-named because, like Beethoven, its proprietor is deaf, the restaurant has a wide repertoir of regional dishes and an extensive list of Rioja wines.

* *Terete*, Lucrecia Arana, 17; Tel. 31 00 23. With its scrubbed wooden tables and baker's oven, Terete is the classical Haro restaurant and always crowded. Its *pièce de resistance* is the *lechazo* (roast baby lamb), but other Riojan dishes, such as the *pimientos rellenos a la riojana* (stuffed peppers), are outstanding. It takes pride in serving the numerous *bodegueros* who patronize it with their own best *reservas*.

Terete's restaurant in Haro

Logroño

As capital of the province of La Rioja, Logroño offers the widest choice of restaurants in the area.

** *Mesón de la Merced*, Marqués de San Nicolás, 136; Tel. 22 06 87. This is the city's most sophisticated and comfortable restaurant and has recently moved from the converted wine cellar in which it was formerly situated to larger premises. Here you will find regional cooking at its most *soigné*, impeccable service and an impressive wine list.

* *San Remo*, Avda. de España, 2; Tel. 23 08 38. Good regional cooking and wines.

* *Carabanchel*, San Agustín, 2; Tel. 22 38 83. Amongst its regional specialities are *menestra de verduras* (mixed vegetable dish), *cabrito asado* (roast kid) and the smoked Idiazábal cheese from the Basque country. Rioja wines.

* *El Cachetero*, Laurel, 3; Tel. 22 84 63. Small, popular and modestly priced with a good selection of Rioja wines.

Other restaurants are *Asador Gonzalez*, *Los Gabrieles* and *Iruña*, while *Robinson's English Pub* is a lively discothèque open until the early hours.

Nájera

San Fernando, Paseo Martín Gamero, 1; Tel. 36 07 00. Handy for the Monasteries of Suso and Yuso, the restaurant serves local dishes such as *pochas riojanas* (beans with *chorizo*), *pimientos riojanos* (stuffed peppers) and *flan* (cream caramel), together with the usual local wines.

Oyón

Mesón de la Cueva, Concepción, 15; Tel. 11 00 22. The Mesón is situated in Oyón, a busy little industrial town some 3 km from Logroño across the River Ebro into the Rioja Alavesa. Housed in a charming old stone-built house, the restaurant offers a variety of regional food. A great speciality is the *morcilla dulce* (see p.000); it also serves a piquant home-made roast *chorizo a la brasa*, with which an excellent accompaniment is a chilled bottle of the young and fruity 'Faustino V' from the adjacent bodega.

San Vicente de la Sonsierra

Hosta Toni, Zumalcárregui, 27; Tel. 33 40 01. This unpretentious and modestly-priced little restaurant is in San Vicente in the Rioja Alavesa, from whose ruined castle one obtains one of the best viewpoints of the Ebro and distant Haro. It features *patatas a la riojana* (potatoes in spicy sauce), *chuletas de cordero* (lamb-chops grilled over vine shoots), curds and young Rioja wines.

Santo Domingo de la Calzada

Parador Nacional de Santo Domingo de la Calzada, Plaza de Santo, 3; Tel. 34 03 00. The Parador, sited in a mediaeval hospice for pilgrims, is perhaps more notable for its surroundings than its cuisine. You may, however, sample a variety of regional dishes in the dining room, and there is a good selection of Rioja wines.

* *El Rincón de Emilio*, Plaza de Bonifacio Gil, 7; Tel. 34 09 90. This is the largest and most popular restaurant in the historic old town of Santo Domingo, a former staging point for pilgrims some 15 km south of Haro. Sunday lunch is an institution. Most modestly priced, it offers a good selection of regional dishes, such as the *menestra riojana* (mixed vegetable dish), *pimientos a la riojana* (stuffed peppers) and *callos a la riojana* (Riojan-style tripe), together with a choice of Rioja wines.

APPENDIXES

1 GLOSSARY OF WINE-TERMS USED IN THE THE RIOJA

NB Terms appearing on labels are separately listed on p.56.

ALAMBRADO	A fine wire mesh used around bottles of *reserva* wines.
APARCERIA	A traditional system of land tenure.
ARROBA	1 A variable liquid measure. 2 A weight of about 25 lb.
ARROPE	A syrup made by evaporating down must.
BARRICA	A wine cask of 225 litres capacity.
BASUQUEADOR	A pole used for breaking up the floating 'cap' in a fermentation vat.
BOCOY	A large barrel of variable capacity; in the Rioja it contains 530 litres.
BODEGA	Literally, a wine-cellar. Used to describe 1 A wine shop. 2 The establishment where wine is made and/or blended and matured. 3 A firm engaged in making, maturing and/or shipping wine.
BOMBA	A pump.
BORRACHA	A wine skin.
BOTA	A small leather wine bag.
BRAZO	One of the main branches of a vine.
CALADO	An underground wine-cellar.
CATADOR	A wine-taster.
CAPATAZ	The cellar-master at a bodega.
CAVA	1 An establishment making sparkling wine. 2 A term used to describe such wine made by the Champagne method.

CAVALTA	The operation of digging around the vines.
CEPA	A wine stock.
CLARO DE HUEVO	An egg-white.
CLARO	Clear.
COLA DE PESCADO	Isinglass.
COMPORTON	A wooden tub of 80 to 120 kg capacity used for transporting the grapes to the bodega.
COÑAC	Spanish brandy.
CONSEJO REGULADOR	The regional supervisory body controlling the making of wines conforming to the *Denominación de Origen*.
COOPERATIVA	A co-operative winery.
CORQUETE	A curved knife used for harvesting the grapes.
COSECHA	Harvest, vintage.
COSECHERO	Owner of a vineyard, often used of the small independent producers.
CRIANZA	The maturing of wine in oak.
CUADRILLA FORASTERA	A group of grape-pickers.
CUBA	A fermentation vat.
CUERO	A wine skin.
CUNACHO	A wicker container for picking grapes.
CUVA	A large barrel of 25,000 litres capacity.
DEGUSTACION	Tasting.
DENOMINACION DE ORIGEN	The guarantee of the Consejo Regulador corresponding to the French *Apellation d'Origine*.
DEPOSITO	A large tank, usually of lined concrete or stainless-steel, for storing or blending wine.
EDUCACION	The maturing and/or blending of new wine.
ELABORACION	The making and further treatment of wine.
EN VIRGEN	The fermentation of wine *en blanc*—without skins, pips or stalks.
ENOLOGIA	The science of wine-making.
ENOLOGICO	An oenologist.
ETIQUETA	A label. For a list of descriptions commonly used on labels, see p. 56.
EXPORTACION	Export.
EXPORTADOR	Exporter, shipper.
GERENTE	The manager of a bodega.
GRANEL, A	In bulk.
GRANO	The berry of the grape.
HECTAREA (HA)	A hectare of 2.471 acres.
HECTOLITRO (HL)	A hectolitre of 22 gallons.
HOLANDAS	Grape spirit containing 65 per cent by volume of alcohol.
HOLLEJO	A grape skin.
GRADO	Degree of alcohol; 13° means 13 per cent by volume.
INGENIERO AGRONOMO	A wine technologist.
INJERTO	A graft.
LAGO	The traditional open stone or cement tank used for fermentation.

LICOR	Liqueur, spirit.
LITRO	A litre of 1.76 pints.
LEVADURA	A yeast or ferment.
MALVINA	A toxic substance found in wines made from hybrid grapes.
MAYORAL	An experienced picker in charge of a *cuadrilla forestal*.
MECADOR	A pole used for breaking up the floating 'cap' in a fermentation vat.
MISTELA	A sweet must in which fermentation has been arrested by addition of alcohol.
MOSTO	Must, the juice extracted from grapes prior to fermentation.
OBRERO	A set day's work in the vineyards.
ORUJO	The skins and pips of the grapes removed before or after fermentation of the must; popularly, *aguardiente de orujo*, a spirit distilled from the *orujo* and resembling the French *marc*.
OBTURADOR	A glass stopper allowing for escape of gas from a cask.
PAGO	The limits of a vineyard.
PELLEJO	A wine skin.
PILA	The small second chamber of a *lago*, into which the new wine is run.
PIPA	A pip.
PODA	Pruning.
PODA EN VASO	The traditional method of pruning in the Rioja, leaving three main stems.
PODON	A curved knife used for pruning.
PORRON	A glass drinking-vessel with a long spout.
PORTADOR	A wooden container for transporting the grapes from a vineyard.
PORTAINJERTO	A resistant stock on which the vine is grafted.
PRENSA	A wine-press.
PULGAR	One of the main stems of the vine.
QUINTAL METRICO	A measurement of weight equal to 100 kg.
RACIMO	A bunch of grapes.
RASPON	A stalk.
REGLAMENTO	The official rules issued by the Consejo Regulador for the guidance of producers and shippers.
SACADOR	A labourer who carries the baskets of grapes from the vineyard.
ROBLE	Oak.
SANGRIA	Aerated red wine with added citrus juice.
SARMIENTO	A wine shoot.
SINDICATO	A trade union.
SOCIO	A Partner in a cooperative winery.
TINA	A large oak vat.
TINO	A large storage cask.

TONEL	A large storage barrel containing several *barricas*.
TONELADA	A metric ton, 1000 kg or approximately 10 hl of wine.
TOLVA	An Archimedean screw used for transferring the fruit to the crusher.
TRASIEGO	The racking or decanting of wine from the lees.
TREN	A bottling line.
TURBIO	Turbid.
UVA	A grape.
VARA	A unit of measurement of 0.87 m used in spacing the plants in a vineyard.
VENDIMIA	The wine harvest.
VID	A vine.
VIÑA, VIÑEDO	A vineyard.
VINICULTURA	The science and practice of wine-making.
VINO	Wine (see also p.00).
BLANCO PARDILLO	A wine made in historical times by mixing a little red wine with white.
COMUN, CORRIENTE	Ordinary wine, *vin ordinaire*.
DE AGUJA	Slightly sparkling, pétillant.
DE CORAZON	The middle portion of wine fermented in a *lago*.
DE LAGRIMA	Wine made from a must separating without mechanical pressure.
DE MESA	Table wine.
DE PASTO	An ordinary beverage wine, often light.
DE YEMA	The wine first drawn off a traditional *lago*.
VIRGEN	Wine fermented without the skins and pips.
VITICULTOR	A wine-grower.
VITICULTURA	The cultivation of vines for wine-making.
ZONA DE CRIANZA	An area within which wines qualifying for *Denominación de Origen* may be mature and blended.

2   *FACTS AND FIGURES*

VINES AND VINEYARDS

Land under vines

Province	*Area*
La Rioja	33,000 ha
Alava	7000 ha
Navarra	4000 ha

Distribution of vine varieties (%)

	Rioja Alta	Rioja Alavesa	Rioja Baja
Tempranillo	60	80	2
Mazuelo	10		
Garnacho	10	5	90
Graciano	2		
Viura	15	10	3
Malvasía	2		
Others	1	5	5

Location of vines

More than 4 million	*Between 2 to 4 million*	
Aldeanueva	Alcanadre	Logroño
Alfaro	Andosilla	Nájera
Arnedo	Briones	Murillo
Ausejo	Calahorra	Oyón
Autol	Elciego	San Vicente
Cenicero	Haro	
Quel	Labastida	
San Asensio	Lapuebla	
Tudelilla	Laguardia	

The most densely-planted areas are those of Alfaro in the Rioja Baja, with 2274 ha, and of Cenicero in the Rioja Alta, with 1472 ha. The highest concentration of Garnacho is in Alfaro and Autol, with 1741 ha; of Tempranillo, in San Vincente de la Sonsierra, with 967 ha; and of Viura, in Cenicero, with 432 ha.

1 hectare averages 2700 vines.

1 vine occupies 3.7 sq m of ground.

1 hectare produces 4000 kg of black grapes (1.48 kg per vine) or 7000 kg of white grapes (2.59 kg per vine).

100 kg of grapes yield 84 kg of must, 13 kg of skins and pips and 3 kg of stalks.

Taking into account losses during racking, etc, 100 kg of black grapes yield 49 litres or 68 bottles of a three year-old wine. On this basis, the yield per hectare of vineyard is 2720 bottles.

Average annual production

	(million of litres)
Red	100
White	20
Rosé	20

Because of a series of poor harvests during the mid-1970s, average annual production over the last ten years has dropped to 110 million litres.

BODEGAS

Numbers of bodegas according to capacity

Capacity (litres)	Type	Number
50,000	Small family-owned	1727
500,000	Medium-sized family-owned and public companies	30
5,000,000	Large family-owned and medium-sized public companies	15
Above 10,000,000	Multi-nationals and large public companies	7
Total number of registered bodegas		2324

Small bodegas are thickest on the ground in the neighbourhood of San Asensio in the Rioja Alta, where there are 207.

3   EXPORTS OF RIOJA, 1982

The table on page 170 shows that, on the basis of imports of bottled Rioja, the leading foreign markets, in order of importance, were Denmark, the United Kingdom and Switzerland. In terms of value, Switzerland was well ahead because of its huge import of wine in bulk. A striking feature of the table is the enormous importance of northern Europe generally as a market for Rioja; the value of wine sold in this area was 69 per cent of the whole.

Figures for the first eight months of 1983 show a change. The United Kingdom, with imports of 2,037,925 litres of bottled wine, has narrowly crept ahead of Denmark, with 1,937,116 litres, while Holland is in third place with 1,418,244 litres. In terms of value, too, taking into account both bottled wine and bulk imports, the United Kingdom is currently the largest purchaser, marginally ahead of Switzerland.

The dramatic rise in Rioja imports in the United Kingdom is illustrated by the following figures:

Year	Number of cases
1976	29,000
1977	87,000
1978	235,000
1979	329,243
1980	193,327
1981	234,953
1982	273,904

On the basis of the first eight months, the projection for 1983 is 340,000 cases.

The exceptionally high figure for 1979 was caused by the large number of Rioja firms shipping to the United Kingdom for the first time. This resulted in overstocking by the trade, which, together with the onset of the world depression, led to a much reduced figure for 1980. Since then there has been a steady increase in imports, and 1983 bids fair to set a new high.

	In bottle (litres)	*In bulk* (litres)	*Total value* (1000 ptas)
Australia	62,351		10,834
Austria	73,947		13,285
Belgium	1,332,132	414,358	220,936
Brazil	96,375		19,142
Canada	638,274		82,536
Denmark	2,886,080	284,231	449,905
Dominica	100,101		19,030
Finland	15,828	490,000	26,855
France	901,072	403,654	157,368
Holland	2,118,522	225,161	312,030
Ireland	127,243		22,205
Italy	62,830		9,570
Japan	269,272	355,222	88,472
Luxembourg	71,240		13,323
Mexico	525,495		148,867
Norway	30,731	346,583	45,191
Panama	66,089		12,923
Puerto Rico	238,872		49,825
Sweden	1,287,808	1,402,853	296,507
Switzerland	2,256,865	5,988,826	737,185
United Kingdom	2,465,140		442,119
United States	2,152,707	460	476,545
Venezuela	1,225,388	34,000	305,574
West Germany	1,877,325	225	312,634
Others	1,014,178	443,200	160,173
TOTAL	21,876,865	9,947,773	4,433,040

BIBLIOGRAPHY

Allen, H. Warner, *A History of Wine* (London, 1961).

Carbonell Razquín, Mateo, *Tratado de la vinicultura* (Barcelona, 1970).

Castillo, José del, *Los vinos de España* (Bilbao, 1971).

DIVO, Le Courrier de Constant Bourquin, special number on the Rioja, Lausanne, 1977.

Editorial Escudo de Oro, *La Rioja, Art Treasures and Wine-growing Resources* (Barcelona, 1981).

Elias, Luis Vicente, *La elaboración tradicional del vino en La Rioja* (Madrid, 1981).

Firestone Hispañia, 1:1,500,000 maps of Spain, No.3.

Ford, Richard, *A Handbook for Travellers in Spain* (London, 1847).

Guia del viajero, Madrid (Banco Exterior), 1982 (English ed., trans, Jan and Carlos Read, *The Traveller's Guide*, Madrid, 1982).

Harper's Wine & Spirit Gazette, export number on the Rioja, n.d.

Huetz de Lemps, A., *Vignobles et vins du nord-ouest de l'Espagne*, 2 vols, (Bordeaux, 1967).

Johnson, Hugh, *The World Atlas of Wine*, 2nd ed., (London 1977); *Wine Companion* (London, 1983).

La Gaceta del Norte, special supplement on Rioja wines (September 1979, Bilbao).

Larrea Redondo, Antonio, *Arte y ciencia de los vinos españoles* (Madrid, 1957); *Vides de la Rioja*, Madrid (Ministerio de Agricultura), 3rd ed., 1978.

Llano Gorostiza, Manuel, *Los vinos de Rioja* (Bilbao, 1973); *Un vaso de bon vino* (Bilbao (C.V.N.E.), 1979).

Manjón, Maite, *Cuisine of Rioja*, in *The Journal of the International Wine & Food Society* (August, 1981).

Marcilla Arrazola, J., *Tratado práctico de viticultura y enología españolas*, Madrid (Vol. I, *Viticultura*, 1963; Vol. II, *Enología*, 1967).

Ministerio de Agricultura (I.N.D.O.), *Catastro vitícola y vinícola de la Rioja*.

    Catastro vitícola y vinícola de Alava.

    Estatuto de la Viña, del Vino y de los Alcoholes, 1970.

    Orden de 1 agosto de 1979 por la que se reglamenta el uso de las indicaciones relativas a la calidad, edad y crianza de los vinos.

    Reglamento de la Denominación de Orígen 'Rioja', 1979.

    Reglamentación de Vinos espumosos naturales y vinos gasificados, 1972.

Peñin, José, *Manual de los vinos españoles*, 3rd ed., (Madrid, 1981); *Manual de los vinos de Rioja* (Madrid, 1982).

Perez, Dionisio (Post-Thebussem), *Guía del buen comer español* (Madrid, 1929).

Rainbird, George, *Sherry and the Wines of Spain* (London, 1966).

Read, Jan, *The Wines of Spain and Portugal* (London, 1973); *Guide to the Wines of Spain and Portugal* (London, 1977); *The Wines of Spain* (London, 1982); *Pocket Guide to Spanish Wines* (London, 1983); *The Century Companion to the Wines of Spain and Portugal* (London, 1983); *The Wines of Spain*, in André Simon's *Wines of the World*, 2nd ed. by Serena Sutcliff, (London, 1981).

Read, Jan, and Manjón, Maite, *Flavours of Spain* (London, 1978).

Reay-Smith, J., *Discovering Spanish Wine* (London, 1976).

Ruiz Hernández, Manuel, *Estudios sobre el vino de Rioja*, Haro, n.d.; *'El Rioja'*, Haro, n.d.

Torres, Miguel A., *Viñas y vinos*, 2nd ed., (Barcelona, 1978); (English ed., *Wines and Vineyards of Spain*, trans. Jan Read, Barcelona, 1982); *Vino español, un incierto futuro* (Barcelona, 1978); *Los vinos de España — Cata* (Barcelona, 1983).

Many research papers on viticulture and viniculture in the Rioja, by Antonio Larrea, Manuel Ruiz Hernández and others, have appeared in the weekly *Semana Vitivinícola*, published in Valencia.

INDEX